God's Daily Word

Jerry Stratton

DEDICATION

I joyfully dedicate this book to my loving wife, Dotse. She is my inspiration as she devotes herself to being the ideal Christian wife, mother, and grandmother. She has demonstrated the true meaning of sacrificial love, and mere words can never describe how precious she is to me and her entire family. We love you, Nana!

CONTENTS

ACKNOWLEDGMENTS

I gratefully acknowledge those who have encouraged me, prayed for me, and advised me during my journey in the ministry. Foremost among these encouragers is my own father, John R. Stratton. As a pastor, he set a worthy example as a humble servant of Jesus Christ and left a legacy of ministry to the needs of others. Thanks, Dad.

Chuckle: *"You're old when you get the same sensation from a rocking chair that you once got from a roller coaster."*

Quote: *"To believe only possibilities is not faith, but mere philosophy."* ~ Sir Thomas Brown

New Year: New Beginning

"In the beginning God created the heavens and the earth" (Genesis 1:1 NLT).

"In the beginning you laid the foundations of the earth, and the heavens are the work of your hands" (Psalm 102:25 NIV).

Genesis 1:1 records the new beginning of all new beginnings. Have you ever wondered why God even bothered to create the heavens and the earth? Did He just need a few more toys with which to amuse Himself? Or did He have in mind a great and amazing master plan to gloriously reveal Himself to mankind, the crown jewel of His creation? The Scriptures tell us it was the later.

Because *"God is Love,"* (1 John 4:16), He wanted someone with whom He could fellowship, share His love, and have that love returned. That someone was to be the zenith of His creation—Adam and Eve—the parents of the human race. He also created an environment in which mankind could exist, grow, prosper, and commune with Him in concert with all creation.

We often think of the New Year as a time of new beginnings. We may want our circumstances to change for the better. We want our problems and challenges to be reduced in size and frequency. We want our love relationships to grow and become more fulfilling.

As you begin this year, what do you plan to do to make your dreams and desires become reality? God took definite action to bring about the beginning He had in mind. Will you be proactive and take positive actions to make this the best year of your life? As we begin this year, let's reflect on the following:

"For God so loved the world that he gave his one and only son, that whoever believes (trusts, has faith) in him shall not perish but have eternal life." (John 3:16).

"... for all have sinned and fall short of the glory of God" (Romans 3:23).

"For the wages of sin is death, but the gift of God is eternal life in Christ Jesus our Lord" (Romans 6:23).

"But God demonstrates his own love for us in this: While we were still sinners, Christ died for us" (Romans 5:8).

"... if you confess with your mouth, 'Jesus is Lord,' believe in your heart that God raised him from the dead, you will be saved. For it is with your heart that you believe and are justified and it is with your mouth that you confess and are saved... for everyone who calls on the name of the Lord will be saved" (Romans 10:9-10, 13).

There is no better time than now for a new beginning. You may need to repent of your sin, give your heart and life to Jesus Christ, and pray to receive Him as Savior and Lord. If you are already a born again believer, it's a great time to commit your life to Him anew and pledge to walk with and serve Him more faithfully.

Jan 02

Chuckle: *Worry is like a rocking chair; it will give you something to do, but it won't get you anywhere.*

Ponder this: *Today is the tomorrow you worried about yesterday and Tomorrow is the day you should not worry about today.*

Do Not Worry

"Do not worry about anything; instead, pray about everything. Tell God what you need, and thank him for what he has done. If you do this, you will experience God's peace, which is far more wonderful than the human mind can understand. His peace will guard your hearts and minds as you live in Christ Jesus" (Philippians 4:6 NLT).

It is easy to find things to worry about these days. The economy, health issues, crime, terrorism, etc., provide us plenty of fodder to feed our worry-prone minds. But as Christians, we need to understand that God's Word tells us not to worry and that worry is the antithesis of faith. Faith is trusting God in all things, but worry indicates a lack of trust and dependence upon Him.

To worry indicates a deficiency in our faith. It indicates that we believe we should have the ability to fix things in our own strength. But when we realize that we can't the temptation is to just continue worrying and fretting about it. There is a difference between genuine concern and worry. Being concerned about something will mobilize us to take some form of positive action, but worry tends to immobilize us and prevent worthwhile actions.

If you are a chronic worrier, I'm sure you have been

amazed by how often many of the "terrible" things you dream up to worry about never come to pass, or are much less severe than you imagined. Because there are so many ruinous effects of worry, Jesus Himself said, *"Therefore I tell you, do not worry about your life, what you will eat or drink; or about your body, what you will wear. . Who of you by worrying can add a single hour to his life. . . Therefore do not worry about tomorrow, for tomorrow will worry about itself"* (Matthew 6:25, 27, 34 NIV).

John Wesley, the eighteenth century Anglican preacher, theologian, and founder of the Methodist movement, had this to say about worry, *"I could no more worry than I could curse or swear."* Oh that each of us Christians could say this about ourselves. Instead, many of us continue to suffer the debilitating consequences of worry and anxiety. These may include damaging our health due to stress, reducing our productivity, negatively affecting the way we treat others, and ultimately reducing our ability to trust in God and His promises.

A great goal for the new year would be—with God's help—to reduce and then finally eliminate worry from our minds. Just think about the happiness and peace we could experience if worry was no longer a dominant factor in our lives.

Jan 03

Chuckle: *Husband: "Do you have any idea how many really great people there are in this country?"*
Wife: "No, I don't, but I'm sure it's one less than you think."
Quote: *"Time wasted is existence; used is life."*
~ Edward Young

Live as If This Year Will Be Your Last

"Show me, O Lord, my life's end and the number of my days; let me know how fleeting is my life. You have made my days a mere handbreadth; the span of my years is as nothing before you. Each man's life is but a breath" (Psalm 39:4-5 NIV).

"What is your life? You are a mist that appears for a little while and then vanishes" (James 4:14 NIV).

I don't mean to be morbid, but it seems appropriate that we should live the new year with a view toward the end of our lives. We would be wise to pause and think about how we would want others to remember us—about what is important in life. I think most of us will want people to remember us as someone who made a difference in the lives of others. Once we've decided how we want to be remembered, we should work our way backwards to the present and start doing those things for which we want to be remembered: loving, caring, serving, giving.

Robert Morris said, *"I hate funerals and would not attend my own if it could be avoided, but it is well for every person to stop once in a while to think of what sort of a collection of mourners he is training for his final event."*

We should live, and let happiness surprise us. Happiness will surprise us if we give ourselves to others. Jesus, in the upper room, wrapped a towel around His waist, took a basin of water, and washed His disciples' feet. He assumed the role of a common servant and said to His disciples, *"I have given you an example, that you should do as I have done for you"* (John 13:15 NIV). Then Jesus concluded, *"Now that you know these things, you will be blessed (happy) if you do them"* (John 13:17).

I believe Jesus knew that happiness is like a butterfly. The more you chase it, the more it flies away and the more elusive it becomes. But if you stay busy serving others, it will light on you unexpectedly. The happiest people are serving people—happiness just sneaks into their lives, sometimes when they least expect it. Real happiness is a by-product of a well lived life as was modeled by Jesus.

The deaf and blind Helen Keller put it this way, *"I find life an exciting business—and most exciting when it is lived for others."*

Danny Glover had this to say, *"We make a living by what we do. We make a life by what we give."* If we live as if this year might be our last by serving others, the new year will be the best year of our lives.

Jan 04

Chuckle: *"Laughing is good exercise; It's like jogging on the inside."*

Quote: *"Prayer can make your week days strong, your trying days triumphant, your Sabbath days sacred, and your holidays wholesome."* ~ William Ward

Post-Holiday Depression

"Come quickly, LORD, and answer me, for my depression deepens. Don't turn away from me, or I will die" (Psalm 143:7 NLT).

Note: *If you suffer from severe depression which affects your ability to carry out normal activities and interact with others, please seek professional medical help.*

Many people experience post-holiday blues, anxiety, and depression after the Christmas and New Year holidays have come and gone. I think it's natural to feel some sort of an emotional let-down after days and weeks of frenzied activities and precious times with family and friends. But others suffer lingering sadness and despondency. Some causes may include:

~ Family Disappointments: The holidays bring precious times of love, joy and exhilaration in healthy family units. However, not everyone is part of a healthy family. Emotional, verbal, and even physical abuse can spoil the otherwise joyous time and lead to broken family relationships which bring sadness and even depression.

~ Financial Problems: Some are saddened because they just couldn't afford to buy gifts for those they love. Others got caught up in the Christmas shopping frenzy and spent more than they could afford. They may have maxed out credit cards as if a day of reckoning would never come. When the bills start coming in, they are jerked back into reality, and begin to worry and fret about how to pay for their spending binge.

~ Severe Loneliness: When our loved ones have left for home and we are left alone, we can experience loneliness, sadness and depression. The elderly may feel depressed both during and after the holidays because they feel neglected, alone and unloved. This can be especially true for those in nursing homes or whose children live far away. It can be a terribly difficult time for those who are spending their first Christmas without spouses and friends who have passed away. They treasure life as they once knew it, and struggle to come to grips with how it is now.

There may be other reasons we feel blue and depressed once the excitement of the holidays has passed. If so, what should we do? For Christians, the solution to such conditions can be found in our relationship with our Lord and loving Christian friends. *"Then Jesus said, "Come to me all of you who are weary and carry heavy burdens, and I will give you rest"* (Matthew 11:28 NLT). Our Lord is willing and eager to grant you His peace and comfort when you turn to Him.

I pray that God will grant you His peace and joy as we minister to one another in times of need. There's no better medicine for our own depression than to bring joy to others by ministering to their needs.

Jan 05

Chuckle: *City slicker: "I finally went for a ride this morning."*
Ranch hand: "Horseback?"
City slicker: "Yep, he got back about an hour before I did."
Quote: *"At any age it does us no harm to look over our past shortcomings and plan to improve our characters and actions in the coming year."* ~ Eleanor Roosevelt

Facing an Uncertain Year

"Trust in the Lord with all your heart; do not depend on your own understanding. Seek his will in all you do, and he will direct your paths" (Proverbs 3:5-6 NLT).
"Do not be anxious about anything, but in everything, by prayer and petition, with thanksgiving, present your requests to God" (Philippians 4:6-7 HCSB).

I'm sure we all wonder what the new year will bring. If you are elderly, you may be concerned about the uncertainty of your health, medical bills, an ailing spouse, or your ability to retain your independence. As a parent, you may be struggling with financial issues as well as issues involving your children, their education, their health, and their struggles as they grow up in a corrupt society. Whatever your age, the new year brings uncertainties as well as exciting challenges and opportunities.
When I fret and worry about the uncertainties of life, I catch myself trusting in my own strength, abilities, and resources. But Jesus told us not to worry or be anxious about anything we may need.
"So I tell you, don't worry about everyday life—whether you have enough food, drink, or clothes. Doesn't life consist of more than food and clothing? . . . Can all your worries add a single

moment to your life? Of course not. . . Why be like the pagans who are deeply concerned about these things? Your heavenly Father already knows all your needs, and he will give you all you need from day to day if you live for him and make the Kingdom of God your primary concern" (Matthew 6:25, 27, 32-33 NLT).

What a simple proposition and promise—yet it is so difficult for many to accept. The point here is that we should make our relationship with God our first priority. Once we've done that, it's amazing how He will remove our worries and anxieties and meet our every need. In our Proverbs passage, we are instructed to trust the Lord with every fiber of our being, and never depend on our own wisdom to handle challenges and problems.

This year no doubt we will feel inadequate to deal with difficult situations as they arise; and often we may feel as if we can't really trust anyone enough to reveal our personal problems. But God knows what is best for us and is a far better judge of what we want and need than we are. As we begin the new year, let's strive to make Him the central and vital part of everything we do. Let's claim His promise to meet our needs and guide us as we do our best to live according to His will and purpose for our lives.

Jan 06

Chuckle: *"Did you hear about the dyslexic Satanist? He sold his soul to Santa!"*

Quote: *"It is our care for the helpless, our practice of lovingkindness, that brands us (Christians) in the eyes of our opponents. 'Look!' they say, 'how they love one another! Look how they are prepared to die for one another!'"*
~ Tertullian (160-225 AD)

A New Kind of Love

Jesus to His disciples, "A new command I give you: Love one another. As I have loved you, so you must love one another. By this all men will know that you are my disciples, if you love one another" (John 13:34-35 NIV).

From the time that Moses received the Old Testament Law from God, the standard for loving others was "love your neighbor as yourself." For the sake of discussion, let's call this *neighborly love.* But Jesus went far beyond neighborly love when He described the kind of love we should have for one another as brothers and sisters in Christ—the kind of sacrificial love He had shown for His disciples and has shown for you and me.

I believe Jesus gave this new command to His disciples because: (1) They had experienced Jesus' love first hand and could now understand the dimensions of that love. (2) They were experiencing a major crisis because their Lord, Teacher, Mentor, and Companion was about to leave them, and they needed a new kind of love for each other to see them through. (3) Soon after His resurrection, Jesus would give them the most awesome task ever given, the Great Commission, to evangelize the whole world. To be successful in this mission, they would need a Christ-like love for each other.

No longer is "love your neighbor as yourself" a sufficient love for Christ's followers. Now we are commanded to love one another in the same way Jesus loves us—a love that is based on Jesus' example, *"As I have loved you, so you must love one another."* The apostle Paul put it this way, *"Be imitators of God, therefore, as dearly loved children and live a life of love, just as Christ loved us . . ."* (Ephesians 5:1-2). This kind of love is unconditional and demands nothing in return.

This love gives credibility to our witness. *"By this all men will know that you are my disciples."* When those we are trying to reach for Christ see us loving one another the way Jesus loves us, our words will ring true and we have credibility. Others will be drawn to Christ by His love.

This love is demonstrated by our actions. *"Dear children, let us love not with words or tongue, but with actions and truth"* (1 John 3:18). This means going out of our way to encourage, strengthen and otherwise help one another. It means placing the welfare of others ahead of our own. It means giving even when it hurts. It means doing whatever is necessary to meet spiritual, physical, and emotional needs of our brothers and sisters in Christ.

It's a love not of our own strength. Loving one another as Jesus loves us is impossible on our own, but is entirely possible when we allow Jesus, in the form of His indwelling Holy Spirit, to love through us. *"I have been crucified with Christ, and I no longer live, but Christ lives in me"* (Galatians 2:20). Allowing Jesus to love through us is dependent upon our love for Him. Jesus said, *"If anyone loves me, he will obey my words"* (John 14:23). If we truly love our Lord, we will obey this "new command."

Jan 07

Chuckle: *"The human brain starts working the moment you are born and never stops until you stand up to speak in public."* ~ George Jessel

Quote: *When you think of the blessings of God, remember one child's description of an elevator: "I got into this little room and the upstairs came down."* ~ Unknown Source

Adversity Brings Blessings

"The apostles left the high council rejoicing that God had counted them worthy to suffer dishonor for the name of Jesus" (Acts 5:41 NLT).

"God blesses the people who patiently endure testing" (James 1:12 NLT).

It is alien to the world's way of thinking to say that adversity and suffering could be reasons for rejoicing. However, sometimes the greatest blessings come out of difficult times. They can deepen your relationship with your Lord and dependence upon Him.

Our passage refers to the beatings Peter and others had suffered. This was the first time apostles had been physically abused for their faith. But to them such abuse was reason for joy. They understood how Jesus had suffered on their behalf and praised God for allowing them to share in that suffering— to be persecuted for their Lord.

When I think about blessings coming as a result of trials and troubles, I'm reminded of the beatitudes. *"Blessed, happy are those who mourn, are persecuted, are insulted."* To be happy and blessed when everything is going wrong requires viewing life from God's perspective. Such blessings come solely from our relationship with Jesus Christ.

The rewards from having Christ in your life can make the adversity and trials of this life appear as insignificant compared to the joy of belonging to Him. For blessings to come from adversity, that adversity must be the result of our faithfulness to our Lord. If trouble comes to us because of our sinful actions, there's no way God can bless us. However, when we suffer trials, persecution, or other hardship because of our loyalty to Christ, He will be with us all the way.

"Dear friends, don't be surprised at the fiery trials you are going through, as if something strange were happening to you. Instead, be very glad—because these trials will make you partners with Christ in his suffering, and afterward you will have the wonderful joy of sharing his glory when it is displayed to all the world" (1 Peter 4:12-13 NLT).

"Be happy if you are insulted for being a Christian, for then the glorious Spirit of God will come upon you . . . it is no shame to suffer for being a Christian. Praise God for the privilege of being called by his wonderful name" (1 Peter 4:14, 16 NLT).

The apostle Paul puts joy and praise into perspective because of God's blessings for His people. *"How we praise God, the Father of our Lord Jesus Christ, who has blessed us with every spiritual blessing in the heavenly realms because we belong to Christ"* (Ephesians 1:3 NLT). Paul wrote in Philippians 3:10, *"I want to know Christ and the power of his resurrection and the fellowship of sharing in his sufferings, . . ."* Someone has said, *"A brook would lose its song if God removed the rocks."*

Jan 08

Chuckle: *In a rural area, a new family called a local official to request the removal of the "Deer Crossing" sign on their road. Their reason was that many deer were being hit by cars and they no longer wanted them to cross there.*

Quote: *"The only difference between the Saint and the Sinner is that every saint has a past and every sinner has a future."* ~ Oscar Wilde

A Saint's Life

"For we are God's masterpiece. He has created us anew in Christ Jesus, so that we can do the good things He planned for us long ago" (Ephesians 2:10 NLT).

You may ask who am I anyway? Do I matter? What is my impact? Where is my place? Do I make a difference? When we are in Christ, we have purpose and we can make a difference in our family, church, community, nation, and the world. In Christ, we are new creations designed to do what God planned for us before we were born.

Perhaps you have never thought of yourself as a saint, but the Bible says we are all saints if we know Christ as Savior and Lord. If God says I am a saint, I should live like one. In Romans 1:7 we read: *"To all in Rome who are loved by God and called to be saints."* The word "saint" means to be holy and set apart unto God as His special possession. As a saint you: (1) have been adopted into God's family; (2) are made holy and blameless; (3) are forgiven of your sins; (4) are sealed by the Holy Spirit; and (5) are the dwelling place of the Holy Spirit.

"The word 'saint' has come far from its original New Testament meaning. When we think of a saint, we think of some

stylized human figure depicted in stained glass, or of a person long dead who has been officially declared as an ecclesiastical relic. However, one of the clearest definitions is 'A saint is a dead sinner, revised and edited,'" ~ Illustrations for Biblical Preaching; Edited by Michael P. Green.

For a meaningful life, we need a mind-set change. We must believe what God says about us, not what others say, or what we say or think. Don't focus on what we were before Christ, but what we are in Christ. *"If anyone is in Christ, he is a new creation; the old has gone, the new has come,"* (2 Corinthians 5:17 NIV).

When ducklings hatch, they bond with whatever is closest. Usually it's with the mother duck. They relate to her, learn from her, and become like her. But I heard about a duck that bonded with a dog. It tried to act and be like a dog. A saint is bonded to Jesus and tries to act and be like Him. A victorious and significant life comes when I focus on what God says I am and begin to focus on being like Jesus. Each of us should say, "I'm a saint (Christian) and I want to live like it."

A little boy attended a church with beautiful stained-glass windows. He'd been told the windows held pictures of Saint Matthew, Saint Mark, Saint Luke, Saint John, Saint Paul, and other saints. One day the boy was asked, "What is a saint?" He replied, "A saint is a person whom the light shines through."

Jan 09

Chuckle: *"Adolescence is that period when a boy refuses to believe that someday he will be as ignorant as his parents."*

Quote: *"Children are the hands by which we take hold of heaven."* ~ Henry Ward Beecher

Joys of Adoption

"His unchanging plan has always been to adopt us into his own family by bringing us to himself through Jesus Christ. And this gave him great pleasure" (Ephesians 1:5 NLT).

To adopt means to take someone into one's family by a legal procedure. There's something about the word "adopted" that stirs a warm feeling within us. When a child is adopted, he or she is accepted, loved, and wanted as part of a family. Being adopted denotes a special bond between the adopters and adoptee. Listen to this touching story.

A new mother stayed with her parents for several days after the birth of her first child. One afternoon she remarked to her mother that it was surprising that the baby had dark hair, since both her husband and she were fair. The grandmother said, "Well, your daddy has black hair." To which the daughter replied, "But Mama, that doesn't matter, because I'm adopted." With an embarrassed smile, that mother said the most wonderful words her daughter had ever heard: "I always forget."

Can you imagine how much her mother's expression of love and acceptance meant to this daughter? Similarly, God has expressed His love for us and says, "I always forget" that sin once kept you from being my child. All Christians are adopted children of God and are accepted by God with the same unconditional love that this mother had for her daughter. In

Scripture, adoption is a relationship conferred by God's act of free grace which redeems each of us from the bondage of sin.

"... God sent his Son, born of woman, born under law, to redeem those under law, that we might receive the full rights of sons (children) ... So you are no longer a slave, but a son (child); and since you are a son (child), God has made you also an heir," (Galatians 4:5-7 NIV).

"Now if we are children, then we are heirs—heirs of God and co-heirs (of God's kingdom) with Christ..." (Romans 8:17 NIV).

Adoption is the legal proceeding whereby a person who is not a child's natural parent becomes the child's legal parent. Adopted children enjoy all the same rights and privileges as biological children. In a similar spiritual way we, as adopted children of God, enjoy God's favor as does His one and only Son, Jesus.

God's intention, and the result of our adoption as His children, is to give us a change in status, which was planned from eternity and brought about by Jesus Christ. The presence of the Spirit of God in our lives is both the instrument and the result of this relationship. Our being chosen as the adopted children of God is solely dependent upon the atoning blood of Jesus Christ and our personal saving relationship with Christ through faith.

Jan 10

Chuckle: *"Marriage is an institution. Marriage is love. Love is blind. Therefore, marriage is an institution for the blind!"*

Quote: *"A bell is not a bell until you ring it; A song is not a song until you sing it. Love in your heart is not put there to stay; Love is not love until you give it away."* ~ Oscar Hammerstein II

Affection of the Strongest Kind

"It is right for me to feel this way about all of you, since I have you in my heart; for whether I am in chains or defending and confirming the gospel, all of you share in God's grace with me. God can testify how I long for all of you with the affection of Christ Jesus," (Philippians 1:7-8 NIV).

Isn't this the most touching expression of love and devotion you've ever read? Here Paul turned from his high expectations for the future to his tender and compassionate love for the Philippian Christians. God's grace had given them a special place in his heart. In my years as a pastor, God brought across my path some of the most precious people in the world. Bonds of love and friendship were developed and continue to this day. I can appreciate the heart of Paul and his love for Christians in Philippi.

Partakers—sharers—of God's Grace: *"It is right for me to feel this way about you, since I have you in my heart . . . all of you share in God's grace with me."* It was unthinkable to Paul that he would fail to express his love and desire to be with the Philippian Christians or to pray for them. As fellow recipients of God's grace, they shared a bond like no other. The Christians in Philippi were not shamed by Paul's imprisonment. Rather, they identified with his cause, and in many ways, participated with him.

In verse 8, Paul expresses his deep yearning to be with them once again. *"I long for all of you."* He compares his love for them to that of Jesus. This deep yearning of Paul to be with his Christian friends serves as an example to all of us. If we say we love one another, why do so many Christians have little or no desire to be together with brothers and sisters in Christ? Some of our greatest joys and blessings should come from spending time together in fellowship and worship. Which of these definitions describes your love for others?

"Infantile love follows the principle: 'I love you because I am loved.' Mature love follows the principle: 'I am loved because I love you.' Immature love says: 'I love you because I need you.' Mature love says: 'I need you because I love you.'" ~ Erich Promm

Paul definitely displayed mature love by first telling the Philippians of his deep love for them which then led to his telling them how he yearned to be with them. What a beautiful picture of the way we should love, need, and enjoy one another.

Jan 11

Chuckle: *"I have this theory that chocolate slows down the aging process.... It may not be true, but do I dare take the chance?"*

Quote: *"Such to me is the new image of aging; growth in self, and service for all mankind."* ~ Ethel Percy Andrus

Aging God's Way

"Is not wisdom found among the aged? Does not long life bring understanding?" (Job 12:12 NIV). *"Children's children are a crown to the aged, and parents are the pride of their children"* (Proverbs 17:6 NIV).

In God's Word there are numerous references to the value and responsibilities of the aged. Many societies around the world hold the elderly in the highest esteem. They are honored, respected, appreciated, and protected with great and tender care. They are recognized for what they can offer in the forms of wisdom, understanding, and insight. I wish it were more so here in our society.

We live at a time when the youthful look is worshiped. People are drawn to all sorts of weird topical compounds, body-building contraptions, weight-loss plans, and even plastic surgery—all touted to make us look younger and more beautiful. With this emphasis on looking young, attractive, and vigorous, we who are growing older sometimes feel as if we're being pushed aside and have little to offer.

We are tempted to think that life is virtually over for us, and that we're being ostracized. If we aren't careful, we can easily allow our self-esteem to slip into the pits. But please don't let our youth-oriented culture put these monkeys on your back. If you're physically able, get up out of that easy chair! Stay active, both physically and mentally. Laugh a lot. Find something useful to do consistent with any physical limitations you may have. You are important to your God and those around you. You can still make a difference in people's lives.

There is so much you can do to make your life and the lives of others better. It all begins with attitude. I've heard that aging is unavoidable, but growing old is optional. When those aches and pains persist we could argue with that conclusion, but there is much truth in it. If we come to the point where we see ourselves as useless, we will likely be useless. But as long as we can face each day with joyful gratitude to God for life and the opportunity to serve Him and others, we will be surprised at the ways God can use us, regardless of our age or physical condition.

If you're a senior adult who feels joy has passed you by, that it's for youth and children, may I suggest you find ways to bring joy to your age-group by your kindness and thoughtfulness. As you bring joy to others, you will experience joy yourself.

Someone has said, *"Esteem age and you will always have life to look forward to. Esteem youth and you proclaim your own obsolescence."*

Jan 12

Chuckle: *"Be nice to your kids. One day they will choose your nursing home!"*

Ponder This: *"I do not pray for success. I ask for faithfulness."* ~ Mother Teresa

Be Strong and Steady

"So, my dear brothers and sisters, be strong and steady (stand firm), always enthusiastic about the Lord's work, for you know that nothing you do for the Lord is ever useless" (1 Corinthians 15:58 NLT).

Do you ever become tired or apathetic toward service to your Lord? Do you become discouraged when faced with the apathy of other Christians? Do you feel you've failed when you don't see the expected results of your labor?

In our passage, Paul says that because of the resurrection of Christ, nothing we do for Him is ever in vain or useless. Everything we do for our Lord for His glory is credited to our accounts and will bear eternal rewards (See 2 Corinthians 5:10). However, sometimes we can become apathetic about our service because we don't see the results we hope and pray for.

As I read this passage, I am reminded that Christ has already won the ultimate victory over sin, death, and the grave, and this knowledge should definitely affect the way I live right now. You should never lose your excitement and enthusiasm for the work of our Lord. You should never become weary or discouraged over an apparent lack of results from your faithfulness, but rather keep on doing the work of the Lord with the assurance that it is not in vain.

"Many years ago a humble pastor served a church in a little

country town. His ministry was quiet, and few souls were brought to Christ there. Year in and year out, the work became more and more discouraging. It was only years later that the faithful minister found great joy in the knowledge that one of those he had won to Christ was Charles Haddon Spurgeon, a man who was later used by God to bring multitudes to his Son. Humble service is rewarded now and certainly will be rewarded even more when Christ comes." ~ Illustrations for Biblical Preaching; Edited by Michael P. Green

Hold on, persevere, be faithful to the trust given you. Take courage and never give up or give in to the temptation to let up in your service to your Lord. You will be rewarded for your faithfulness in God's own time. Reflect on the hope you have in Christ and what He's done for you. Such reflection will remind you of God's amazing love and Christ's amazing sacrifice that atoned for your sins and gave you the assurance of eternal life. Serving Him out of love and gratitude should be the desire of our lives.

Jan 13

Chuckle: Kid's comments on angels: *"Angels don't eat, but they drink milk from Holy Cows!"* ~ *Jack, age 6*

Quote: *"The trouble with opportunity is that it's always more recognizable going than coming."* ~ Unknown source

Acknowledging Jesus Publicly

"If anyone acknowledges me publicly here on earth, I will openly acknowledge that person before my Father in heaven. But if anyone denies me here on earth, I will deny that person before my Father in heaven" (Matthew 10:32-33 NLT).

In many evangelical Christian churches, an invitation/commitment time occurs at the end of each worship service. This is to give people the opportunity to respond to God's appeal by making a public profession of their faith in Jesus Christ as Savior. Jesus does not intend that our relationship with Him be kept secret, but He requires a public acknowledgment of our allegiance to Him. During His earthly ministry, every person that Jesus called to follow Him was asked to do so publicly. Jesus expects us to let other people know we are followers of Christ.

This is a serious issue in a society where keeping our religious beliefs private is seen as desirable by some. Many do not think our Christianity should be acknowledged at work, school, or in any other public venue. There is a concerted effort by some to remove the very mention of God in all public government funded places. Yet we must understand what our Lord expects of us as Christians. When we share our faith one-on-one with others, we acknowledge our Lord in the most direct and fruitful way. Of course, as we acknowledge Christ before men, we must do so with the same love and compassion that Jesus displayed as He drew people to Himself.

We acknowledge our Lord by living according to God's holy standards and reflecting Christ's love in everything we do and say. And public acknowledgement of our Lord, by being His witnesses, brings His promises of eternal rewards. Those rewards, however, should not be our primary motivation for being witnesses for Christ. We should do so out of obedience and heartfelt love and gratitude, because of who He is and for what He has done for us. We should do so out of great, unconditional love for those who need to know Him as Savior and Lord.

"A Christian's life should stand out to the world as different. We should be like zebras among horses. When our lives are indistinguishable from the world's, we are like albino zebras. They really are zebras, their parents were zebras, they know they are zebras on the inside. But to all who see them from the outside they are no different from horses." ~ Unknown source.

Jesus said, *". . . let your light shine before men, that they may see your good deeds and praise your Father in heaven"* (Matthew 5:16 NIV).

Jan 14

Chuckle: *Clerk: "This jug is genuine Indian pottery."*
Customer: "But it says, 'Made in Cleveland.'"
Clerk: "Haven't you ever heard of the Cleveland Indians?"
Quote: *"Anger would inflict punishment on another;*
meanwhile, it tortures itself." ~ Publilius Syrus

An Angry Jesus

"He looked around at them in anger, and (was) deeply
distressed at their stubborn hearts . . ." (Mark 3:5 NIV).

Anger, in human terms, usually refers to selfish, destructive feelings—a strong annoyance and a desire to fight back when someone hurts us or opposes us. Such feelings can lead to harmful and objectionable behavior. However, the anger of God is the response of His holiness to the sinful actions of people. When God takes action against sin, it is called "wrath." In the Old Testament, the word translated as "divine anger" is used 177 times, but the word "anger" is rarely used in the New Testament. Our focal passage is one of those instances. Let's focus on what angers Jesus and how He reacts when angry.

We are told in Scripture that Jesus was without sin (see 1 Peter 2:22 and Hebrews 4:15). However, He did become angry on occasion. In our passage we see Jesus' angry reaction after being criticized for healing a man on the Sabbath. The Matthew and Luke accounts of this event leave out the word anger, apparently because they were unwilling to ascribe to Jesus this "human" emotion. But the kind of anger Jesus felt is revealed by His being *"deeply distressed, grieved, at their stubborn, hardened, hearts."*

Another instance where Jesus showed strong emotions,

and even anger, was when He witnessed the actions of the Temple merchants and money changers. *". . he overturned the tables of the money-changers and the seats of those who sold pigeons (sacrificial animals). He said to them, It is written, 'My house shall be called a house of prayer, but you make it a den of robbers'"* (Matthew 21:12-13 NIV). Here Jesus is reacting to the desecration of the holy temple as a place of worship and the injustices against worshipers. He showed God's righteous indignation.

Anger is a normal human emotion. However, it can lead to sin when we become angry for the wrong reasons and we act in sinful ways. Anger becomes a sin when we allow it to fester until it causes us to become bitter and act in ways harmful to others and/or reflects unfavorably on Jesus Christ and Christianity. *"In your anger do not sin. Do not let the sun go down while you are still angry, and do not give the devil a foothold"* (Ephesians 4:26-27 NIV).

Jesus became angry for the right reasons—sinful behavior and injustice. Likewise, we should be indignant and even angry when we see people being mistreated, abused, or neglected. Such anger or indignation should motivate us to do everything we can to correct injustice. However, becoming angry to the point of offensive behavior is never justified.

Jan 15

Chuckle: *Two boys were walking home from church after hearing strong preaching on the devil. One said to the other, "What do you think about all this Satan stuff?"*

The other boy replied, "Well, you know how Santa Claus turned out. It's probably just your Dad."

Quote: *"Faith consists in believing when it is beyond the power of reason to believe. It is not enough that a thing be possible for it to be believed." ~ Francois Voltaire*

Ambassadors for Christ

"We are Christ's ambassadors, and God is using us to speak to you. We urge you, as though Christ himself were here pleading with you. 'Be reconciled to God!'" (2 Corinthians 5:20 NLT).

The word "ambassador" is used to describe envoys sent by governments to other nations as special representatives, messengers, and interpreters. Our government appoints ambassadors to countries with whom we have diplomatic relations to represent our interests, to explain, interpret, and promulgate the values of the United States, and to serve the American citizens living in those countries. In our passage the word applies to us as representatives of Christ charged with carrying His message of God's redeeming love and His plan for reconciling sinners to Himself.

As believers, we are God's ambassadors, sent into the world with His gospel message of Jesus Christ. This is an awesome and important responsibility, and one that should never be taken lightly. When we speak it is as if God is speaking through us. The Holy Spirit empowers our words and convicts the hearts of those to whom we speak representing Christ. Really, we are allowing God to use us as conduits through whom the gospel message is communicated. Our message is clear: Be reconciled to God through faith in Jesus Christ! The news of reconciliation is not merely good news, but urgent news, entailing consequences of the greatest eternal importance for all people.

A final thought: An ambassador never substitutes his own personal message for the message of the one who sent him or her. We must never alter, water down, or substitute our own words for those of our Heavenly Father. When an ambassador loses his focus and loyalty to the one he represents, he is no longer an ambassador. Likewise, when an ambassador does not accurately convey the message of the One who sends him, he or she becomes a hindrance to God's kingdom work. The message of reconciliation can be summarized as follows:

"For God made Christ, who never sinned, to be the offering for our sin, so that we could be made right with God through Christ" (2 Corinthians 5:21 NLT).

Jan 16

Chuckle: *Teacher: "What happened in 1809?"*
Eddie: "Abraham Lincoln was born."
Teacher: "Right. Now what happened in 1812?"
Eddie: "He turned three years old."
Quote: *"Let not him who is houseless pull down the house of another, but let him work diligently and build one for himself, thus by example assuring that his own shall be safe from violence when built." ~ Abraham Lincoln*

The Evils of Envy

"A heart at peace gives life to the body, but envy rots the bones" (Proverbs 14:30 NIV).
"Love is kind. It does not envy, . ." (1 Corinthians 13:4 NIV).
"Keep your lives free from the love of money and be content with what you have, . ." (Hebrews 13:5 NIV).

From Wikipedia: Envy is an emotion which "occurs when a person lacks a superior quality, achievement, or possession and either desires it or wishes the other does not have it. . ."

From the dictionary: Envy is "jealousy and dislike felt toward another because he has some thing, quality, etc., that one would like to have."

It seems to me that materialism and envy go hand in hand. In a society where one's worth is measured by what one has, the insatiable desire to "have" can drive a person into sinful thoughts and actions toward those who may have more than he. Envy is the enemy of contentment, and causes us to lose the joy we should have in the life God has given us.

Today's quote is from a speech Abraham Lincoln made to a labor union in 1864. I'm sure he was aware that a person's hopes can easily turn to envy and hate toward someone because those hopes have been realized by another.

Hopes and aspirations are great if accompanied by a willingness to work to fulfill those hopes in a way that honors God. However, the envious often want what someone else has without the willingness to work for it. Some may even feel entitled to have what they desire. Our passages teach us some valuable lessons and we should let them sink into our hearts. This fable reveals a great truth about envy.

Satan was angered by the incompetence of his subordinates because they had failed to draw a holy man into sin. He said, "You have failed because your methods are too crude. Watch this."

Satan approached the holy man and whispered in his ear, "Your brother has just been made Bishop of Alexandria." Instantly the holy man's face showed Satan had been successful: a great scowl formed over his mouth and his eyes tightened up. "Envy," said Satan, "is often our best weapon against those who seek holiness." ~ Illustrations for Biblical Preaching; Edited by Michael P. Green.

"A little grit in the eye destroyeth the sight of the heavens; and a little malice or envy, a world of joy." ~ Thomas Traherne

Jan 17

Chuckle: *An insurance man was teaching his daughter to drive. Suddenly the brakes failed. "I can't stop," she wailed. "What should I do?"*

"Don't panic," her father told her. "Just hit something cheap!"

Great Quote: *"If you think you can walk in holiness without keeping up perpetual fellowship with Christ, you have made a great mistake. If you would be holy, you must live close to Jesus."*
~ Charles Haddon Spurgeon

Are You Prepared?

"So be prepared, because you do not know what day your Lord is coming. . . You must be ready all the time. For the Son of Man will come when least expected" (Matthew 24:42, 44 NLT).

How would you change your life if you knew Jesus would return tomorrow? This is an all important question for each of us. In our passage, Jesus tells us that His coming will be both unpredictable and unexpected; therefore, we should be prepared to meet Him at all times. The promise that Jesus will return to earth came from the lips of Jesus Himself.

This precious promise gives all Christians great joy and comfort from knowing our Lord will return to claim His church and usher in the events leading to our spending eternity in His presence in a place the Bible calls heaven. The following quotation sheds additional light on this glorious event.

The New Testament writers speak of Christ's returning, "soon" or "quickly," with the apparent expectation that he might return in the writer's own lifetime. However, the meaning of returning "soon" is that it would happen "at any moment." It is like my phone answering machine. The message informs the caller that I am away from my desk but will return "soon." I use

the same message whether I expect to be gone two minutes or two weeks, for the very simple reason that I want to encourage the person without revealing exactly how long I will be gone!
~ Illustrations for Biblical Preaching; Edited by Michael P. Green

Yes, Christ's return for His own will be both sudden and swift. When it happens, the opportunity to prepare for His return will have passed. Our preparations should be made now while there is still time. First, we should repent of our sins and ask Jesus Christ to come into our lives as Savior and Lord. Then we should live each day in such a way that we welcome His coming with excitement and anticipation. I heard someone say that we should never do anything for which we would be ashamed if Jesus came while we were doing it. The apostle Paul wrote, *"Remember, the Lord is coming soon"* (Philippians 4:5b NLT). Jesus said, *"See, I am coming soon, and my reward is with me, to repay all according their deeds"* (Revelation 22:12 NLT). When He comes, our ultimate joy will be fully realized. He who gave Himself for us, and whose Spirit lives within us will have kept His promise and fulfilled His final purpose for us.

Jan 18

Chuckle: *A little boy found a leaf pressed between the pages of an old family Bible. "Mom," he called, "look what I found! It's Adam's clothes!"*

Quote: *"When a man realizes that he is a beloved child of the Creator of all, then he is ready to see his neighbors in the world as brothers and sisters." ~ Robert Runcie, Archbishop of Canterbury*

Be Accommodating to Others

"If someone forces (compels) you to go one mile, go with him two miles. Give to the one who asks you, and do not turn away from the one who wants to borrow from you" (Matthew 5:41-42 NIV).

Among the meanings of the word "accommodate" is *"to fit in with someone's wishes or demands in a helpful way."* In our passage, the words of Jesus remind us of our obligation to go the extra mile to be accommodating to others when they compel us to do something or ask a favor of us. The same principle applies when we become aware of a need that we have the resources to meet.

If we're too busy or indifferent to the needs of others, we may turn down their cries for help. Or we may reluctantly do what someone requests of us, but nothing more; just enough to satisfy the request and clear our consciences. Jesus tells us to do more than is requested or expected.

We may have our day completely planned out with no time to spare, and then God brings someone across our path with a request that would require us to change our plans to meet the need. According to Jesus' words, in our passage, what should be our attitude?

Even though it may be inconvenient at times to go the extra mile, doing so can be the key to success in your business, your marriage, your church, or other relationships. I'm sure you've come face to face with a rigid, uncaring, unyielding, or an unaccommodating person. What is your reaction to that person?

Our Lord has instructed Christians to put others ahead of our personal desires or plans, even when it is inconvenient and costs us valuable time, effort, and other resources.

Jesus expands the teaching of accommodation in Luke 6:27-36, where He tells us to love our enemies, turn the other cheek, and give to anyone beyond what they ask. To me, the message for Christians is to always do the unexpected in the eyes of the secular world. He wants us to show that our ability to love and respond to others is unlimited, in the same way God's love for us is unlimited. Returning good for evil and going the extra mile will give credibility to our witness for our Lord. Jesus teaches us to be accommodating to others in all circumstances, even to our enemies.

"And if you do good to those who are good to you, what credit is that to you? Even sinners do that. . . . But love your enemies, do good to them, and lend to them without expecting to get anything back. Then your reward will be great, . ." (Luke 6:33, 35 NIV).

Jan 19

Church bulletin blooper: *"Irving Benson and Jessie Carter were married on October 24 in the church. So ends a friendship that began in their school days."*

Quote: *"No one does well what he doth against his will."* ~ *St Augustine of Hippo*

Being Accountable

"So then, each of us will give an account of himself before God" (Romans 14:12 NIV).

"Whatever you do, work at it with all your heart, as working for the Lord, not for men, since you know that you will receive an inheritance from the Lord as a reward" (Colossians 3:23-24 NIV).

To be accountable means to be liable or responsible for one's actions. Accountability seems to be in short supply these days. Some are unwilling to accept blame for their inappropriate and negligent actions, while being quick to claim the credit for things that turn out well—even when the credit rightly belongs to others. To be accountable, we must first accept personal responsibility for our actions.

When you accept responsibility, you automatically place yourself in a vulnerable position and risk catching the blame as well as the praise. But until you are willing to accept the risks of responsibility, you will not be willing to be held accountable. This is true in the secular professional world, as well as in the work of our Lord.

What about you and me? Are we willing to step forward and be held accountable for our lives and the ministry challenges God has placed before us? When you walk the walk of faith, you will eagerly accept being held accountable before

God. You will accept responsibility with an attitude of humility and without fear of failure, because you are dependent upon the Holy Spirit of God to guide you, sustain you, teach you, and strengthen you. It is to Him that you and I are ultimately accountable.

"For we must all appear before the judgment seat of Christ, that each one may receive what (reward) is due him for the things done while in the body, whether good or bad" (2 Corinthians 5:10 NIV).

Until you conquer the fear of failure and its ensuing criticisms, it will be difficult to muster the courage to be what God wants you to be in your professional life or your spiritual life. As Christians, we should be the best employees and the best managers in the workplace, and the most faithful and inspirational workers and leaders in our churches and communities, for the glory of our Lord. Practicing accountability now will ensure a joyous experience when we are held accountable at the judgment seat of Christ.

"When God's work is done in God's way for God's glory, it will never lack God's supply. God is not obligated to pay for our selfish schemes. He is obligated to support His ministry."
~ Hudson Taylor

Jan 20

Chuckle: *The five year-old asked her preacher dad why he bowed his head before preaching.*

"Well, Honey," he said, "I'm asking God to help me preach a good sermon."

"How come He doesn't answer you?" she asked.

Daily Quote: *"The invisible thing called 'GOOD NAME' is made up of the breath of numbers that speak well of you."* ~ Lord Halifax

A Good Name

"A good name is more desirable than great riches; to be esteemed is better than silver and gold" (Proverbs 22:1 NIV).

Our reputations are determined by the choices we make and the ensuing actions those choices precipitate. Each waking moment of every day, we are confronted with situations requiring decisions that will impact our lives either positively or negatively in the eyes of those who know us, and through whom our reputations are established.

The choice with eternal consequences is what you decide to do when confronted with the truth of God's love and His plan for the salvation of your eternal soul through faith in Jesus Christ. Once you decide to trust Him as Savior and Lord, and begin your walk of faith with Him, important life decisions must continue to be made every day.

As we travel down the road of faith, we find it has many paths. At each split in the road, the decision you make will help determine your reputation as a Christian. Robert H. Schuler put it this way: *"At each fork in the road, we should ask this question. 'Where do I want to go?' 'Which road will take me there?' Be careful which road you choose."*

Our passage provides important guidance for making life's decisions by placing relative values on the outcomes. *"A good name is more desirable than great riches."* But we know our modern society tends to view the accumulation of wealth as the true measure of success. That's why it is so important to ask these questions: "Where do I really want to go in this life? What is the best decision to take me there?" Does the desire to please God and have a good name drive your decisions, or does the desire for personal gain trump any concern for God's will or your good name?

My last daily quote speaks powerfully to me at this point. *"Each of us will one day be judged by our standard of life, not by our standard of living; by our measure of giving, not by our measure of wealth; by our simple goodness, not by our seeming greatness."* ~ William Arthur Ward

Today each of us will make many choices. Some will seem relatively insignificant, while others may determine your entire future. Often concern for one's good name is sacrificed on the altars of self-centeredness and self-gratification. But for the Christian, each decision should be made prayerfully and with great care. The choices we make reveal our true character. *"Your ideal is what you wish you were. Your reputation is what people say you are. Your character is what you are."*

Jan 21

Chuckle: *A man wrote to the IRS: "I have been unable to sleep knowing that I cheated on my income tax. I understated my taxable income and have enclosed a check for two hundred dollars. If I still can't sleep, I will send the rest."*

Quote: *"The road is always better than the Inn."*
~ Cervantes

Arrival: A Starting Point

"I have fought a good fight, I have finished the race, and I have remained faithful. And now the prize awaits me—the crown of righteousness that the Lord, the righteous judge, will give me on that great day of his return. And the prize is not just for me but all who eagerly look forward to his glorious return" (2 Timothy 4:7-8 NLT).

During my thirty years of military service, I remember thinking, "If I can just get that promotion, I'll be happy; if I can get that great assignment, I'll find fulfilment; if I can only reach my retirement date, I'll feel as if I have reached my ultimate goal and will be content."

But I learned that every goal achieved in life is only a starting point for something better, not a final destination. During my 28 years of ministry, I have come to realize that my greatest joy and satisfaction comes from the daily journey with my Lord. Each achievement along the way brings a brief moment of satisfaction, but more importantly, it provides inspiration and motivation to continue the journey.

The apostle Paul could have been satisfied with what he had accomplished at any point along his missionary journeys. But he recognized full well that his happiness and satisfaction would never be fully realized until he completed his voyage and was in the presence of his Lord receiving the award that God had in store for him.

He could have been content with his accomplishments in Antioch, Ephesus, or Philippi and could have made any of them his final destination—mission accomplished. However, his greatest joy was the continuing drive to become more like his Lord Jesus.

We can spend our time wishing for a status in life to give us joy and contentment. But I've found it's better to enjoy the present, and to savor life's experiences along the road toward that goal. Our desire should be to faithfully continue the journey to become more like Him. *"I press on toward the goal to win the prize for which God has called me heavenward in Christ Jesus"* (Philippians 3:14 NIV).

Look back over your life and I'm sure you will see that every goal achieved, or every event experienced along the way, has been instrumental in molding you into the person you are today. In our quote, Cervantes must have been saying, "As attractive as the inn is for a weary traveler, it is the journey, not the inn, that brings the most satisfaction and happiness. The inn is only a starting point for the remainder of the excitement."

"I have learned to take each inn along the way with the traveler's stride—not as a stopping point, but as a starting point for some new and better endeavor." ~ Maurice Maeterlinck

Jan 22

Chuckle: *The judge looked sternly at the two men in his court and asked, "Can't this case be settled out of court"?*

One of the men replied, "Your honor, we were trying to do that when the police came."

Quote: *"If we have not quiet in our minds, outward comfort will do no more for us than a golden slipper on a gouty foot."*
~ John Bunyan

Be Still and Know

"Be still (silent, quiet), and know that I am God" (Psalm 46:10 NIV).

"Step out of the traffic! Take a long, loving look at me, your High God, above politics, above everything" (Psalm 46:10 MSG).

Just saying the words "be still" or "stillness" is calming and soothing to our minds and bodies. But I must admit, I'm not very good at just being still. Are you? If we are like most people these days, our lives are in a constant state of hustle and bustle. We feel as if we're always behind the power curve.

We may not be getting enough sleep. We may be constantly running out of time before we exhaust our lists of things we think need to be done. We may find it increasingly difficult just to find stillness, peace, and quiet. We all need some down time in a restful oasis where we can put down our burdens and refresh our minds and hearts.

In our passage, God tells His people to take time each day to be still and quietly consider who He is, and to exalt/honor Him. He further says, *"I will be exalted among the nations, I will be exalted in the earth."*

When we step back from the frustrations and cares that beset us and spend some quiet time reflecting on God's love, mercy, grace, and forgiveness, we will want to fall at His feet with thanksgiving and adoration. Then He will affirm that He is the Almighty and has everything under control.

Just think how comfortable you feel when you know everything that bothers you is being taken care of—when you become aware that everything is going to be alright. When we trust in our Lord, everything *will* be alright.

When we begin to grasp the power and sovereignty of Almighty God, we want to serve Him and learn more of Him each day. Today, be still and focus your heart and mind on God; and His presence will become increasingly real to you. His power will protect you and give you peace even in times of turmoil and uncertainty.

Heart surgeon Michael E. DeBakey once observed: *"For me, the solitude of early morning is the most precious time of day. There is the quiet serenity that disappears a few hours later with the hustle and bustle of the multitude. Early morning hours symbolize for me a rebirth; the anxieties, frustrations, and woes of the preceding day seem to have been washed away during the night. God has granted another day of life, another chance to do something worthwhile for humanity."*

Jan 23

Chuckle: We have a group of preachers in our town who bowl. They call themselves "Holy Rollers!"

Quote: *"If he has faith, the believer cannot be restrained. He betrays himself. He breaks out. He confesses and teaches this gospel to people at the risk of life itself."* ~ Martin Luther

Ashamed of the Gospel?

"I am not ashamed of the gospel, because it is the power of God for the salvation of everyone who believes" (Romans 1:16 NIV.)

Romans was written to the Christians in Rome by the apostle Paul, an intelligent and articulate man totally committed to his calling from Christ Himself. He presents the case for the gospel message clearly and forthrightly in his letter to all believers in Rome—and to us. Even though the persecution of Christians was commonplace during the time of Paul's ministry, he never wavered in his zeal and commitment to unashamedly spread the gospel wherever he went.

Around the world today, hostility and violence against Christians is rapidly increasing. They are being slaughtered, imprisoned, flogged, and otherwise persecuted simply for pledging their allegiance to Jesus Christ. Sadly, most free-world governments and Christians seem largely indifferent to what is happening to our fellow Christians.

In the United States, we do not face the extreme persecutions described above. Yet there is a growing undercurrent of anti-Christian sentiment steadily being revealed. In light of this and the world situation, what should we do as Christians?

What we should not do is to be afraid or ashamed to share

the gospel of Jesus Christ. If you are ever tempted to stop proclaiming this gospel when faced with opposition or persecution, please remember what the gospel—Good News— is all about. It is the power of eternal salvation for anyone who believes. It is the most important message Jesus has commanded us to proclaim. What an awesome responsibility our Lord has given us—to make disciples of all people. In sharing the good news, there is no place for timidity or shame in the hearts of believers.

As we faithfully proclaim the gospel message in today's environment, we must do so with Christ-like love and compassion for all people. The most effective way to demonstrate such love is by our joyful service to others, especially those with extraordinary physical, emotional, or spiritual needs.

James says, *"Show me your faith without deeds, and I will show you my faith by what I do"* (James 2:18b NIV). Someone has said something like this, *"Preach the gospel everywhere you go; and, when necessary, use words."* Our actions often speak louder and more effectively than our words. We can never earn salvation by doing good things, but good deeds of service show that our commitment to God is real and verify our faith in Jesus Christ.

Finally, Jesus said, *"If anyone is ashamed of me and my words, the Son of Man will be ashamed of him when he comes in his glory . . ."* (Luke 9:26 NIV).

Jan 24

Chuckle: *The judge said to the defendant, "I thought I told you I never wanted to see you in here again."*

"Your Honor," the criminal replied, "that's what I tried to tell the police, but they wouldn't listen!"

Quote: *"The control center of your life is your attitude."*
~ Unknown Source

Controlling Our Attitudes

"Why am I discouraged? Why am I sad? I will put my hope in God! I will praise him again—my Savior and my God" (Psalm 42:11 NLT).

Each morning when we rise, each of us has choices to make that will determine the kind of day we will have, and the kind of attitude will we display as we interact with others. We can choose to be discouraged, pessimistic, grumpy, and down-in-the-mouth, or we can choose to rejoice in the Lord and expect a wonderful day in His presence. *"This is the day the Lord has made; let us rejoice and be glad in it"* (Psalm 118:24 NIV).

Making such choices may not always be easy, especially if you are suffering from a physical problem or facing a difficult and challenging day. But only you and I can make such choices. You may not always have control of your circumstances, but you always have complete control of your attitude. When we have trouble with our attitudes it's usually because we are thinking only of ourselves. "Woe is me" is a prevalent attitude of the pessimist because "it's all about me" and my problems.

The apostle Paul had this to say about our attitudes: *"Each of you should look not only to your own interests, but also to the interests of others. Your attitude should be the same as that of*

Christ Jesus" (Philippians 2:5 NIV).

Paul goes on to describe how Jesus humbled Himself and took on the very nature of a servant. If you're feeling sorry for yourself, try focusing your attention on the needs of others and what you can do to help. Happiness is somewhat like a butterfly. When you try to chase it down, it's elusive, but when you go about your business with a healthy attitude, it will often light on your shoulder when you least expect it. With the right attitude, happiness will find you without your having to search for it.

Each morning, try praising God and focusing your attention on the One who can turn all your adverse circumstances around according to His will, or give you the strength and courage to see you through them. When you choose a positive and upbeat attitude, you will be ready to affect the kind of day you'll have. Just meditate on our Lord and what He has done, and continues to do for you, and He will help steer your attitude.

Jan 25

Chuckle: *"Give me a sentence about a public servant," said a teacher.*

The small boy wrote: "The fireman came down the ladder pregnant."

The teacher took the lad aside to correct him. "Don't you know what pregnant means?" she asked.

"Sure," said the boy confidently. "It means carrying a child."

Quote: *"There is nothing that can help you understand your beliefs more than trying to explain them to an inquisitor."*
~ Frank Clark

Between Belief and Unbelief

Immediately the boy's father exclaimed, "I do believe; help me overcome my unbelief!" (Mark 9:24 NIV).

I'm sure there have been times when you longed for God to meet a need in your life—when you knew God had done similar miracles as recorded in the Bible, but somehow you just couldn't quite believe He would do it in your case. Have you prayed for God to do a certain thing, but you really didn't think God would do what you asked? Quite often there's a big difference between our believing God can do something and believing He *will* do something.

The faith spoken of in the Bible is an attitude of complete trust and confidence. If your faith is wavering and you find yourself doubting that God will keep His promises, you may have slipped into the void between belief and unbelief. But we must never forget that even our faith and ability to believe are gifts from God. In our passage, the father recognized a basic truth—we all need God to help us overcome our unbelief.

Listen to what James says about unbelief when praying for

wisdom. *"When you ask him, be sure that you really expect him to answer, for a doubtful mind is as unsettled as a wave of the sea that is driven and tossed by the wind. People like that should not expect to receive anything from the Lord. They can't make up their minds. They waver back and forth in everything they do"* (James 1:6-8 NIV).

Here James makes the point that if we're asking anything from God, we must believe He will give it to us. Our faith must be solid and sure.

If our faith is weak and we have difficulty trusting our Lord in all things, we may have forgotten a basic tenet of our faith—that God can be trusted. Ask God to help you overcome your unbelief and lack of faith. In the same way God has shown His power throughout history, He will work in your life. But we mustn't waver. We must truly believe that God will do even the impossible.

Jesus said, *"Listen to me! You can pray for anything, and if you believe, you will have it"* (Mark 11:24 NLT).

This amazing statement presupposes that our prayers will be for God's will to be done, not ours. When we pray according to the will of the Father, He will answer.

Jan 26

Chuckle: *A father told his teenage son that if he brought his grades to a B average, studied the Bible, and got a haircut, then he would talk about the boy using the family car. After six weeks, the dad said to the son, "I've noticed your grades are up and you're studying the Bible. but you haven't had your hair cut."*

The boy said, "Dad, as I studied the Bible, I noticed that Samson had long hair, John the Baptist had long hair, Moses had long hair... and there's strong evidence that even Jesus had long hair."

The dad replied, "Did you also notice that they walked everywhere they went?"

Quote: *"O God, make us children of quietness, and heirs of peace."* ~ St. Clement

Calm During the Storms

"Last night an angel of the God whose I am and whom I serve stood beside me and said, 'Do not be afraid, Paul, you must stand trial before Caesar, and God has graciously given you the lives of all who sail with you'" (Acts 27:23-24 NIV).

Those who sail the high seas are constantly reminded that they are at the mercy of elements totally beyond their control. They prepare to deal with storms as best they can while recognizing and respecting the risks involved.

Life is like that. We know storms will come into our lives, but God has given us instructions on how to prepare for and deal with them. Jesus said, *"In this world you will have trouble. But take heart! I have overcome the world"* (John 16:33 NIV). When we recognize that our lives are in God's hands, and in faith trust Him in all situations, we can enjoy a sense of calm and peace regardless of the severity of the storms that buffet our lives.

In our passage, we learn that when threatened by harsh storms, the sailors and soldiers with Paul were in a state of panic. But Paul's relationship and fellowship with his Lord allowed him as God's servant to remain calm and at peace. God's promise and Paul's faith allowed him to maintain serenity, and lead and encourage others.

Storms provide the true test of our relationship with God. It's easy to have faith and trust God when we experience smooth sailing, but when the seas of life become rough and threatening, we can be calm because we rely on God's presence and trust in His promise. Can God use your calm and peaceful demeanor to influence others as you pass through the storms in your life?

A hurricane is a storm with cyclonic winds greater than 74 m.p.h. But there is a place of perfect calm in its center—the eye. So it is with us in the storms of life. With the Lord as our center, there is calm and peace, even during the darkest of times and the harshest of storms. Jesus said to His disciples; *"Peace I leave with you; my peace I give you. I do not give to you as the world gives. Do not let your hearts be troubled and do not be afraid"* (John 14:27 NIV).

Chuckle: *One worker to another: "How long have you been working here?"*

Answer: *"Since they threatened to fire me."*

Quote: *"Forgiveness is not an occasional act, it is a permanent attitude."* ~ Martin Luther King

Forgiving Ourselves

"Everyone who believes in him (Jesus) will have their sins forgiven through his name" (Acts 10:43).

I believe our ability to forgive ourselves of things in our past is dependent upon our understanding and acceptance of God's forgiveness. The Bible tells us in many places that God will forgive us of our sins and cleanse us if we believe (trust, have faith) in Jesus Christ. It tells us that our sins will be removed as far as the east is from the west and that they will be remembered against us no more.

Of course, we know that this forgiveness is dependent on our confessing our sins with an attitude of remorse and repentance, asking God to forgive us. *"If we confess our sins, he is faithful and just and will forgive us our sins and cleanse (purify) us from all unrighteousness"* (1 John 1:9 KJV).

Some accept the truth that God forgives the sins of others, but have difficulty believing that God could ever forgive them. They may say, "I've done some pretty terrible things in my life; how can God ever forgive me?" They may feel they don't deserve God's forgiveness.

If you think your sins are just too awful for God to forgive, you'll never be able to forgive yourself. If you can't accept the fact that God will forgive you, that sense of guilt and shame for your past mistakes will continue to haunt and control your life.

This guilt can take away your peace, joy, and assurance of God's love and the love of others. You may feel you do not deserve to be loved either by God or by other people. Such a mind-set can lead to depression, self-pity, and withdrawal from those who love you most.

We must learn to believe God when He promises complete forgiveness, regardless of the dimensions of our sin. You may not feel forgiven, but you must take God at His Word that His forgiveness is complete. Remember that Jesus paid the penalty for your sins by shedding His precious blood on Calvary's cross. If you know Christ as Savior and Lord, your sins are covered by His atoning blood sacrifice. To doubt God's ability, or willingness, to forgive your sins is to put limits on God's power and to belittle His promises.

If you know Christ as Savior, *"You are holy and blameless as you stand before him without a single fault"* (Colossians 1:22). God says, *"No matter how deep the stain of your sins, I can remove it. I can make you as clean as freshly fallen snow"* (Isaiah 1:18). Take God at His word. Trust Him and accept His forgiveness. Then ask Him to give you the strength to forgive yourself as He has forgiven you. Accept God's forgiveness and let go of the past—then your joy will return!

Jan 28

Chuckle: *"I was walking on the beach with friends when one of them shouted, "Look at that dead bird!"*
Someone looked up at the sky and said, "Where?"
Quote: *"This day we sailed on. Course WSW."* ~ Christopher Columbus

Sail On—Don't Give Up

"Consider it pure joy, my brothers, whenever you face trials of many kinds, because you know that the testing of your faith develops perseverance. Perseverance must finish its work so that you may be mature and complete, not lacking anything" (James 1:2-4 NIV).

Most of us are somewhat aware of that famous voyage, in 1492, of three small ships: the Nina, Pinta, and Santa Maria. But I dare say that few of us have an appreciation for the challenges which faced Christopher Columbus and his three crews on that historic first voyage across the Atlantic. According to Wikipedia, this voyage led to the first lasting European contact with the Americas, inaugurating a period of European exploration, conquest, and colonization that lasted for several centuries. Listen to this brief account:
"Our quote for today is the entry which, day after day, Columbus put down in the private log of his first voyage across the uncharted North Atlantic. He must have written it in a spirit alternating between blind hope and quiet despair. Conditions were about as adverse as possible. Storms had damaged the little caravel; the Pinta had lost her rudder; the crews of all three vessels were threatening mutiny; and probably Columbus' own confidence in what seemed an insane enterprise was wavering. But he had set his course in the direction which his own intuition

and logical intelligence let him to believe was the right one, and with dogged courage he kept going." ~ Cornelia Otis Skinner

I see a correlation between this story and the real-life challenges facing a Christian who has set his course as a devoted follower of Jesus Christ, but finds himself beset by trials and obstacles of many kinds. If he or she is not totally committed to Christ and the course they have set, they will find many reasons to turn back and abandon their journey. I'm sure Columbus had anticipated difficulties on his dangerous voyage; however, his strong commitment and conviction kept him from throwing in the towel and turning back.

Do you sometimes get discouraged in your walk with our Lord? Do the challenges and burdens of life become just too great? Here are two additional passages. Jesus said, *"In this world you will have trouble. But take heart! I have overcome the world"* (John 16:33b NIV).

"Dear friends, do not be surprised at the painful trial you are suffering, as though something strange were happening to you" (1 Peter 4:12 NIV).

These verses stress the certainty that troubles will come. It's "when," not "if," we face the inevitable pain, but a positive outlook will help us be joyful as we focus on the good that troubles can produce in our lives. No one enjoys trials, but those who endure them with strong faith will reap the benefits of perseverance, proven character, and hope. Someone said, *"A brook would lose its song if God removed the rocks."* Sail on. . . .

Jan 29

Chuckle: *"If you think you're too small to have an impact, try going to bed with a mosquito."* ~ *Anita Roddick*

Quote: *"The most evident token and apparent sign of true wisdom is a constant and unconstrained rejoicing."* ~ Michel de Montaigne

Rejoice Every Day

"This is the day the Lord has made. We will rejoice and be glad in it" (Psalm 118:24 NLT).

I've heard people say, "I'm just not a morning person," or "Don't bother me in the mornings; I'm a grouch."

Others say, "I love the early morning, and enjoy the beauty of God's creation coming alive at daybreak." Some rejoice at the prospect of another day of life, love, and service to family and others.

Obviously, our own personal temperaments and personalities have a lot to do with the way we greet each new day. But there is a basic truth from God's Word—each new day we live is a gift from God and should be treasured with thanksgiving and rejoicing.

You may say, "But Jerry, you don't understand; the way things are going in my life, I just don't feel like celebrating. I have nothing to be happy about." Oh, yes you do if you know Jesus Christ as Savior and Lord.

Obviously, there are days when we don't feel much like rejoicing. You may be facing yet another day of unemployment; another day of caring for a sick parent or child; another day of struggle with your own health; or another day of heartbreak in a relationship. You may feel like Charlie Brown, pondering his plight in life: *"Yesterday, for one brief moment I was happy. But just when I thought I was winning in the game of life, there was a flag thrown on the play and life dealt me a blow."*

When the psalmist penned the words of our passage, he understood that even when life has dealt us a blow, when our mood is down, when our situation seems out of hand, or when our sorrow and guilt are overwhelming, God can still give us reason to rejoice.

If you can't see any reason to rejoice, be honest with God in your prayers. Take your depression, sadness, and hurt to the one who said, *"Come to me, all you who are weary and burdened, and I will give you rest"* (Matthew 11:28 NIV).

The psalmists were always honest with God and did not hesitate to express their sorrows, anxieties, fears, and doubts. Invariably, when they opened their hearts honestly before God, they came away from that encounter with reasons to rejoice.

When you don't feel like rejoicing, express your feelings to our Lord and let Him show you all the reasons you have to rejoice each and every day. When you look at each day as another gift from God and another opportunity to live and serve Him, you will be glad and rejoice at what God has done for you through Jesus Christ.

Jan 30

Chuckle: *"It's always darkest just before dawn. So if you're going to steal your neighbor's newspaper, that's the time to do it."*

Quote: *"Storms make oaks take deeper root."*
~ George Herbert

Step Out of the Boat

"'All right, come,' Jesus said. So Peter went over the side of the boat and walked on the water toward Jesus" (Matthew 14:29 NLT).

Our passage is from one of the most revealing accounts of faith, doubt, fear, and trust in the entire New Testament. Jesus' disciples were in a boat crossing a lake on a stormy night. About three o'clock in the morning, they were terrified by a figure walking toward them on the surface of the water. After Jesus assured them that it was really Him and not a ghost, Peter asked to be invited to walk on the water toward Jesus. Jesus told him, *"Come."*

God both causes and allows storms in our lives, and always with a purpose. There are storms designed for correction, like Jonah experienced when he disobeyed God by refusing to go to Nineveh as God commanded. Then there are storms of instruction, like the one here in our passage. Peter took a step of faith by stepping out of the boat.

By the way, in Scripture only Jesus and Peter walked on water. By getting out of the boat, Peter was learning to trust God and to grow in his faith. But when Peter took his eyes off Jesus and saw the deep dark water and high waves, his human doubts and fears immediately replaced his faith, and he began to sink.

What a powerful lesson for us. By keeping our eyes on Jesus, our faith will sustain us in every storm of life. Peter became terrified and shouted, "Save me Lord!"

Instantly Jesus reached out His hand and grabbed him. *"You don't have much faith,"* Jesus said. *"Why did you doubt me?"* Here Jesus used the occasion to instruct Peter in what it means to have faith—to trust your Lord in all circumstances.

Although we may start out with good intentions to do something God has asked us to do, sometimes, like Peter, our faith may falter and we become insecure and afraid. But this doesn't mean ultimate failure. Notice that Peter, in his weakness, reached for the hand of Jesus, the only one who could help him. He was afraid, but he looked to Jesus for strength. When we become apprehensive and doubtful during the storms of life, we can remember that Christ has promised to be with us always. He is the only one who can help us.

Because of this adventure on a dark stormy lake, Peter experienced Jesus in a new and powerful way. No matter what storm confronts you, just get out of the boat and trust Jesus. We may be tempted to be critical of Peter for his lack of faith, but remember, he had the faith to get out of the boat.

Jan 31

Chuckle: Headline read: *"Local High School Dropouts Cut in Half!"* Chainsaw Massacre all over again?

Quote: *"Every sunrise is a new message from God, and every sunset is His signature."* ~ William Arthur Ward

Greater Things

"Jesus said to His disciples: I tell you the truth, anyone who has faith in me will do what I have been doing. He will do even greater things than these, because I am going to the Father" (John 14:12 NIV).

This is one of the most profound and amazing declarations to come from our Lord's mouth. What is the truth Jesus wants us to understand from this passage? Surely He doesn't mean we will do greater miracles than raising people from the dead or the granting of eternal life. These miracles are as amazing as they get.

The key lies in Jesus' statement as to why He said we will do greater things than He did while He was here on earth. This will be true *"because I am going to the Father."*

How did His going to the Father change what believers are able to do? It was the coming of the Holy Spirit into the lives of all believers who provides the motivation, direction, and power for us to do greater things. Later Jesus said, *"Unless I go away (to the Father), the Counselor, Holy Spirit, will not come to you; but if I go, I will send Him to you"* (John 16:7 NIV). You see, after Jesus had gone the disciples would be working in the power of the Holy Spirit which would enable them, and us, to carry the Good News of God's Kingdom from Palestine to the entire world.

"But you will receive power when the Holy Spirit comes on

you; and you will be my witnesses in Jerusalem, and in all Judea and Samaria, and to the ends of the earth" (Acts 1:8 NIV).

Jesus' earthly ministry was confined to a relatively small geographical area. It is through the Holy Spirit empowering faithful witnesses, beginning with the Twelve, that His message has gone global. I believe the spread of Christianity around the world constitutes the "greater things" to which Jesus referred.

Down through the ages untold millions have been drawn to faith in Jesus Christ by faithful witnesses and the wooing of the Spirit as He exercises His power to redeem sinners and grant the assurance of eternal life. Our Lord wants each of us to be faithfully and actively involved in doing "greater things" in the power of the Spirit.

Feb 01

Chuckle: *"One way to improve your memory is to lend people money!"*

Quote: *"To love as Jesus loves; that is not only the Lord's precept, it is our vocation. When all is said and done it is the one thing we have to learn, for it is perfection."* ~ René Voillaume

Love As Jesus Loves

"Don't just pretend that you love others. Really love them. Hate what is wrong. Stand on the side of the good. Love each other with genuine affection, and take delight in honoring each other" (Romans 12: 9-10 NLT).

When Jesus was about to go to the cross, He said to His disciples, *"So now I am giving you a new commandment: Love each other. Just as I have loved you, you should love each other. Your love for one another will prove that you are my disciples"* (John 13:34-35 NLT).

When you take our two passages together, a beautiful picture is revealed about how we should love our Christian brothers and sisters—brotherly love. Jesus knew His followers would need a special kind of love for each other to see them through the crisis of His terrible crucifixion and later to carry out the Great Commission to evangelize the world (Matthew 28:19-20).

Previously, Jesus had taught that the standard for loving others was to "love your neighbor as you love yourself." But He knew this kind of neighborly love, would be inadequate for His followers in loving each other. Here Jesus sets a new standard of brotherly love for believers. Now we are to love other Christians not as we love ourselves but as Jesus has loved us.

This is the unconditional sacrificial "agape" love. This is the love Jesus had for us as He gave Himself for us. This kind of love will motivate us to love believers, our neighbors, and all others as Jesus has loved us.

Have you noticed that we often tend to treat total strangers with greater kindness than those closest to us—in our biological families as well as our spiritual/church families? You see, it is our love for each other that proves to the world that we belong to and are followers of Jesus Christ.

Jesus assumes that people will see our acts of love for each other. If they don't see our acts of love for each other, how will they know we belong to Christ? We cannot limit our expressions of love to the four walls of the church. Rather we show our love in our homes, our work places, our classrooms, and everywhere we go each day. Let's examine our hearts and see if we genuinely love one another as Jesus has loved us or if we are just pretending. It's easy to say we love someone, but the genuineness of our words is proven by our actions.

Feb 02

Chuckle: *Why did the bowlegged cowboy get fired? He couldn't keep his calves together!*

Quote: *"We may easily be too big for God to use, but never too small."* ~ D.L. Moody

Love as a Practice

"... serve one *other in love*" (Galatians 5:13 NIV).

Have you ever wondered why we call a physician's work a "practice?" I don't think any of us want a doctor "practicing" on us. We want him to attend to us only after he has perfected his skills. Of course we understand that in this case the word "practice" means he is applying his skills for the benefit of his patients. However, when it comes to Christian love, we need to practice it day in and day out in a life-long effort to get it right—to love as Jesus loves.

Most Christians are pretty good at expressing their love to one another verbally, or maybe even with a hug. Such expressions are rooted in warm and fuzzy feelings we have for our brothers and sisters in Christ. Telling others that we love them is a good thing and should never be neglected. But words alone just won't cut it when we apply the Biblical standard to the way we should love one another.

Christian love is more than words and more than a warm emotional feeling. Christian love is serving the ones whom we love. It is demonstrated by our actions. It means getting our hands dirty as we help meet the needs of others. It means having the heart of a servant like our Lord who wrapped Himself in a towel and washed the feet of His disciples (see John 13:1-17). Jesus set the bar extremely high for us when it comes to loving one another through acts of kindness and service. While none of us has reached the point where we can love like Jesus loves us, we must never stop striving to be like Him. Jesus said, *"As I have loved you, so you must love one another"* (John 13:34 NIV).

> *You know Lord how I serve you*
> *with great emotional fervor,*
> *in the limelight.*
> *You know how eagerly I speak for you,*
> *at a women's club.*
> *You know how I effervesce when I promote*
> *a fellowship group.*
> *You know my genuine enthusiasm at a Bible study. But how would I react, I wonder, if you pointed to a basin of water, and asked me to wash the calloused feet of a bent and wrinkled old woman, day after day, month after month, in a room where nobody saw, and nobody knew?* ~ Ruth Harms Calkin

Feb 03

Chuckle: *A reporter said to a 99 year-old fisherman, "I hope I can come back next year for your 100th."*

"Can't see why not, young man," the old fisherman said. "You look healthy enough to me."

Quote: *"There is a net of love by which you can catch souls."* ~ Mother Teresa

The Dimensions of Love

"Love never gives up, never loses faith, is always hopeful, and endures through every circumstance" (1 Corinthians 13:7 NLT).

I like our passage in The Living Bible: *"If you love someone, you will be loyal to him (or her) no matter what the cost. You will always believe in him (or her), always expect the best of him (or her), and always stand your ground in defending him (or her)."* Genuine unconditional love is totally unselfish and always wants the best for the one who is the object of that love. Let's discover the dimension of love this verse contains.

If you love someone, you will never give up on him or her. Aren't you thankful that Jesus never gave up on you? If we truly love someone, we will be completely loyal to that person regardless of the disappointments and heartaches we may experience. We will encourage rather than condemn—build up, never tear down.

If you love someone, you will never lose faith in him or her. Jesus proved that He believes in you and values you so much that He was willing to sacrifice Himself for you. You are worth all it cost Him on the cross. He has faith in you that His sacrifice will not be in vain, and that you will be faithful in sharing His love and message of salvation with others. Your expressions of faith in someone is a major source of encouragement.

If you love someone, you will always expect the best from him or her. This loving expectation always sees the best in others. It looks beyond the rough surface and sees the great potential in that person you love. This expectation includes the hope that a loved person will live up to the potential given them by our Lord. It looks past the faults and frailties and sees the good in a person.

If you love someone, you will always defend him or her. Love always defends others being subjected to unfair treatment and unwarranted criticism and insults. We will never abandon someone we love, even when their actions are less than lovable. Our defense of them may not be for their actions, but for their priceless value to us as the object of our unconditional love.

These dimensions of love remind us of the love God has for us, and of our inability to love unconditionally without the help of God's Spirit within us. This kind of love goes against our natural inclinations. It manifests itself in our ability to put aside our natural selfish desires and love others without expecting their love in return. The closer we walk with our Lord and the more like Him we become.

Feb 04

Chuckle: *"Why do we put suits in a garment bag and put garments in a suitcase?"*

Quote: *"An individual's highest fulfilment, greatest happiness, and widest usefulness are to be found in living in harmony with His (God's) will."* ~ John D. Rockefeller, Jr.

Love: What Is It?

"This is how we know what love is: Jesus Christ laid down his life for us. And we ought to lay down our lives for our brothers" (1 John 3:16 NIV).

Here the word "love" is translated from the Greek word *"agape."* This kind of love can be defined as "God's kind of love"—the kind of love that caused Jesus to sacrifice Himself for us on a horrible Roman cross. This love is characterized by actions, not mere words. What did John mean when he said we ought to lay down our lives for our friends? Fortunately, it is unlikely that most of us will be required to give our physical lives for someone else as Jesus did for us. Nevertheless, it seems John is saying we Christians should be willing to do so if called upon.

"It is our care for the helpless, our practice of lovingkindness, that brands (Christians) us in the eyes of many of our opponents. 'Look!' they say. 'How they love one another! Look how they are prepared to die for one another'" ~ Tertullian

You wouldn't hesitate to give your life for someone you love dearly—like your spouse or your child. Soldiers lay down their lives for their country and often sacrifice themselves to save their buddies. But is this what John is suggesting we do? Not really. There are many other ways we can lay down our lives for brothers and sisters. Immediately after saying that we ought to lay down our lives for our brothers, John talks about using our material possessions to meet the needs of others.

"If anyone has material possessions and sees his brother in need but has no pity on him, how can the love of God be in him? Dear children, let us not love with words or tongue but with actions and in truth" (1 John 3:17-18 NIV). Then John lets the heavy hammer fall: *"This is how we know that we belong to the truth (Christ), and how we set our hearts at rest in his presence whenever our hearts condemn us. For God is greater than our hearts, and he knows everything"* (1 John 3:19-20 NIV).

This is how we will know that we have been saved and belong to Christ—if we love and meet the needs of our brothers and sisters. Up in verse 17, the word translated "pity" actually means to "shut out" or "close the door." If we see someone in need and shut the door of our hearts toward him, how can the love of God be in us? We can say kind words to someone in need, but do nothing to meet his or her need and our hearts will condemn us for such a lack of agape love—a love of actions.

In light of these passages, are we inclined to feel sorry for someone in need, and maybe share some words of encouragement with him/her, or are we willing to lay down our lives and sacrifice something to meet his/her needs? *"This is how we know that we belong to the truth (Jesus)."* Love is what God is all about and what we should be about.

Feb 05

Chuckle: *Adam said to his wife, "Eve, I wear the plants in this family!"*

Quote: *"Love of God and love of created things are contrary the one to the other; two contraries cannot exist in one and the same person."* ~ St John of the Cross, Ascent I

Love for the Father

"Stop loving this evil world and all that it offers you, for when you love the world, you show that you do not have the love of the Father in you" (1 John 2:15 NLT).

Loving the things of our evil world is sometimes called worldliness. When we think of worldliness, we tend to focus on behavior—acting in a worldly or sinful way, as demonstrated by the people with whom we associate, the places we frequent, or activities we enjoy. But loving the world begins as a condition of the heart which manifests itself in three basic attractions: lust for the gratification of our physical desires; longing for what is appealing to the eye—materialism; and pride in one's importance or status. It was in these same three areas that Satan tempted Adam and Eve in the garden; and he used the same tactics again when tempting Jesus in the wilderness (see Matthew 4:1-11).

On the other hand, those who truly love God also exhibit certain characteristics in their lives: They have unconditional love for others. They display a generous spirit. They are dedicated to humble service. They exercise self-control. They continually seek to know God better each day. Their focus is on God and His kingdom. God's values have become their values.

The ways of the world are totally contrary to God and His

ways, and each of us must decide daily whether to love the world or our heavenly Father. We cannot love both—we must choose one or the other. Jesus said, *"No one can serve two masters. Either he will hate the one and love the other, or he will be devoted to the one and despise the other. You cannot serve both God and money"* (Matthew 6:24 NIV).

Sadly, some "Christians" try to impress others by visibly avoiding worldly attractions and pleasures, while at the same time harboring worldly desires, attitudes, and values deep within their hearts. We may be able to fool other people, but we can never fool our heavenly Father who knows everything about us, even the deepest and darkest secrets of our hearts.

It's obvious that God desires us to love Him, as revealed in the "Great Commandment—*"Love the Lord your God with all your heart and with all your soul and with all your mind"* (Matthew 22:37 NIV). If we faithfully obey this commandment, our desires and love for worldly attractions will fade into our distant memory. Let's ask ourselves: What values are most important to me? Do my actions reflect the world's values or God's values? Do I love God or the world? We cannot have it both ways!!

Feb 06

Chuckle: *"When you don't know what to do, walk fast and look worried!"*

Quote: *"Love is the only force capable of transforming an enemy into a friend."* ~ Martin Luther King

Love Your Enemies

Jesus said: *"You have heard that the Law of Moses says, 'Love your neighbor and hate your enemy.' But I say, love your enemies! Pray for those who persecute you! In that way, you will be acting as true children of your Father in heaven . . . If you love only those who love you, what good is that? Even corrupt tax collectors (sinners) do that much. If you are kind only to your friends, how are you different from anyone else? Even pagans do that. But you are to be perfect (mature), even as your Father in heaven is perfect"* (Matthew 5:43-47 NLT).

At the time of Jesus' ministry here on earth the Jewish people were oppressed under the rule of the Romans. Now imagine yourself in their place—and along comes Jesus to tell God's people to love their enemies. Obviously such teaching could not be accepted by everyone and many turned away from Jesus. Likely their biggest problem was dealing with the definition of love from Jesus' point of view. They thought He was telling them to have warm and fuzzy emotional feelings of affection for their oppressors and enemies. But in reality, Jesus was talking about an act of will. In the same way God despises sin but loves the sinner, we are to love our enemies even though we may detest their actions. If we can understand this, loving our enemies makes more sense.

It takes a conscious effort and submission of will to love

those who mistreat you and always act with their own best interests in mind. We can pray for them and think of ways to make their lives better. Jesus had this attitude toward everyone, even though people hated Him, persecuted Him, and even crucified Him. As the Roman soldiers were killing Him, and people stood around with approving looks, Jesus said from the cross, *"Father, forgive them for they do not know what they are doing."* We are to follow His example of unconditional love and forgiveness. Jesus never stops loving us no matter how much we rebel against His love and ignore His invitation to accept Him by faith for forgiveness of our sins.

What about the last sentence in our passage? *"But you are to be perfect (mature), even as your Father in heaven is perfect."* Jesus is telling His followers—including us—that we are to be different. We are to become perfect or mature Christians as we allow God's Holy Spirit to give us a spiritual makeover. As we allow Him to mold us and shape us into the likeness of Christ, we will display these marks of spiritual maturity:

(1) In character: Here on earth we will never become flawless, but we can strive to become more like Christ every day we live.

(2) In holiness: We are to be submissive to God's desires rather than our own and carry His love and mercy into the world—even to those who hurt us.

(3) In maturity: Achieving Christ-like character and holy living does not happen overnight, but is a growth process over a lifetime of Christian service.

(4) In love: We can learn to love others as completely as God loves us—even our enemies.

Feb 07

Chuckle: *After being punished for losing his temper, a little boy asked his mother, "Can you explain to me the difference between my foul temper and your worn nerves?"*

Quote: *"The heart benevolent and Kind The most resembles God."* ~ Robert Burns 'A *Winter Night'*

Love Is Patient and Kind

"Love is patient, love is kind. . . It is not easily angered" (1 Corinthians 13:4-5 NIV). *"But the fruit of the Spirit is love, . . . patience, kindness . . ."* (Galatians 5:22 NIV).

All too often as Dotse and I sit down to enjoy a meal together, or settle into our easy chairs to read or watch television, the phone begins its relentless ringing. Often it's those pesky, inconsiderate telemarketers trying to sell us something we don't want or need; and they are reluctant to take "no" for an answer. Signing up for the "no call" list has been only partially effective. It's very irritating and makes me want to snarl at the person on the other end in a rush of anger. I'm tempted to become impatient, unkind, rude, and insulting.

However, when I stop to think and seriously consider the situation, I begin to feel guilty and embarrassed because of my attitude. I'm reminded that the person making the call is probably a decent human being just trying to make a living in a tough job market. From my military days, I remember hearing something like this, "If you don't like the bad news message, it does no good to shoot the messenger." After all, the messenger and the telemarketer do not deserve to be treated rudely and suffer the results of our rage. Telemarketing is their job. It should not define who they are, or their value in our eyes, because they are certainly as precious in the eyes of our Lord as you and I.

In our passage, the apostle Paul describes the characteristics of genuine love. Have you thought about loving a telemarketer or someone else that irritates or inconveniences you by their words or actions? God's kind of love is all about others and is directed outward, not inward toward ourselves. Earlier I described my natural inclinations to react in an unkind and unloving way. So how can we love even the telemarketers as Jesus loves us (John 13:34)? I think this quote from the NLT Life Applications Study Bible says it all:

"This kind of love goes against our natural inclinations. It is impossible to have this kind of love unless God helps us set aside our own natural desires so that we can love and not expect anything in return. Thus, the more we become like Christ, the more love we will show to others."

Our passages tell us love is patient and kind and is not easily angered. Such love and patience are fruits of the Holy Spirit living within us (see Galatians 5:22). So the next time a telemarketer or some other person irritates you and you are inclined to react in anger—stop, take a deep breath, and let the Spirit of Christ direct your words and actions. Thus, you will honor God.

Feb 08

Chuckle: *"The most difficult years of marriage are those following the wedding."*

Good Quote: *"Happiness grows at our firesides and is not to be picked in strangers' gardens."* ~ Douglas Jerrold

Love in Marriage, Part 1

"May the Lord make your love increase and overflow for each other and for everyone else, just as ours does for you" (1 Thessalonians 3:12-13 NIV). *"Husbands, love your wives, just as Christ loved the church and gave himself up for her"* (Ephesians 5:25 NIV). *". . . and the wife must respect (and love) her husband"* (Ephesians 5:33b NIV).

A few years ago, Tina Turner had a hit song called, *"What's Love got to do With It."* This song describes many couples today. Marriages are coming apart at an ever increasing rate. Not only that, but the social stigma once attached to divorce and breakdown of the family unit no longer exists. Sadly, growing numbers of children are being abused and abandoned.

Most problems within the family begin and end with the relationship of the husband and wife. What is it that causes so many marriages to come apart? Many reasons are given, but the most serious problem may be a growing lack of understanding of what it means to genuinely love someone. At least three kinds of love should be present in marriage:

1. Romantic Love (Eros): This love describes the sensual attraction of a man and a woman to each other. This "romantic love" is on the level of instincts. It is the chemical reaction of a male to a female, and vice versa. This physical attraction is important but should be only the first step in a growing and

much deeper kind of love. Marriages based *only* on this dimension of love are doomed to disappointment and disintegration once the physical attraction becomes less intense.

2. Respect Love (Phileo): This is brotherly or friendship love, and is based on someone's worth, faithfulness, and reliability. It's the love between friends. It is extremely important that a husband and wife genuinely like each other and be best friends—that they provide each other someone to share their innermost thoughts without fear of rejection or condemnation.

3. Help Love (Agape): This is the highest and noblest form of love. God showed this kind of love when He *"so loved the world that He gave His only Son."* This kind of love sees something infinitely precious in the object of this love. It is a sacrificing love without thought of self, and is not dependent upon circumstances. It is an unconditional selfless love. The other person's well-being becomes more important than your own.

Happy indeed is the home where the husband and wife are romantically attracted to each other. Happier still is the home where the husband and wife also respect each other and are best friends. But the happiest home is the one where every thought and activity is saturated with self-sacrificing "help" love. When love has reached this level a marriage will last a lifetime.

Feb 09

Chuckle: *The Sunday school teacher asked, "Now, Johnny, tell me, do you say prayers before eating?"*

"No Sir," he replied. "We don't have to. My mom is a good cook!"

Quote: *"If we love people, we will see them as God intends them to be."* ~ Unknown Source

Love in Marriage, (Part 2)

"May the Lord make your love increase and overflow for each other and for everyone else, just as ours does for you" (1 Thessalonians 3:12-13 NIV). *"Husbands, love your wives, just as Christ loved the church and gave himself up for her"* (Ephesians 5:25 NIV). *"... and the wife must respect (and love) her husband"* (Ephesians 5:33b NIV).

In Paul's second letter to the Thessalonians, he commended them because their love for one another was increasing. It is God's will that we grow in love for each other. Paul also reminds us that husbands are to love their wives so much that they would be willing to die for them as Christ died for His church. This degree of love should flow both ways in the family circle. Let's look at some ways you can help your love to grow for your family.

(1) Appreciate the fact that God loves each member of your family as much as He loves you. *"For God so loved the world"* means He loves equally the husband, wife, son, daughter, brother, sister, parent, grandparent. We need to love each member of our families because of their infinite worth in God's sight. The next time you look into the face of your wife, husband, or child, think about how precious she/he is to God.

As you consider the value of your family members in God's eyes, their worth increases in your eyes.

(2) Have a healthy love and respect for yourself. If you do not appreciate and respect yourself according to God's instructions, it will be impossible for you to properly love and appreciate your spouse and others. When Jesus told us to *"love your neighbor as yourself,"* He was affirming a healthy love for ourselves. However, Paul tells, *"Do not to think more highly of ourselves that we ought..."* (Romans 12:3 NIV). If you suffer from low self-esteem (sense of worth/value), you will look at others in the same way. As you recognize how precious you are to God, it will help you to respond to the truth that God loves and values each of your family members equally.

(3) Practice loving your family with actions, not just words. One of the most difficult things to give away is kindness, for it's usually returned in more than full measure. *"A pastor was kind to a young lady in his congregation. Later she made for him a beautiful plaque that contained the letters TALK in vertical order, with the beautiful message below it, 'Try A Little Kindness.'"* It was her way of saying "thank you" for his kindness.

How long has it been since you tried a little kindness on your marriage partner? Your children? Your parents? Those closest to us deserve our most expressive acts of kindness—expressions of love that even the deaf can hear and the blind can see.

Feb 10

Chuckle: *"My wife and I were at a "Dude Ranch" in Texas. The cowboy preparing the horses asked if she wanted a Western or English saddle, and she asked what the difference was. When he told her one had a horn and one didn't, she replied, 'The one without the horn is fine. I don't expect we'll run into too much traffic.'"*

Quote: *Often the difference between a successful marriage and a mediocre one consists of leaving about three or four things a day unsaid."* ~ Harlan Miller

Love in Marriage, Part 3

"Be kind and compassionate to one another, forgiving each other, just as in Christ God forgave you. Be imitators of God, therefore, as dearly loved children and live a life of love, just as Christ loved us and gave himself up for us . . ." (Ephesians 4:31-5:2). *"Husbands, love your wives, just as Christ loved the church and gave himself up for her"* (Ephesians 5:25 NIV). *". . . and the wife must respect (and love) her husband."* (Ephesians 5:33b NIV).

Last time we began exploring some ways to help your love to grow for your family. These included: (1) Recognizing and appreciating the fact that God loves each member of your family as much as He loves you. (2) Having a healthy love and respect for yourself. (3) Practicing loving your family with your actions rather than words.

Today we continue with: (4) Increasing love in your family as you practice forgiveness. It is inevitable that family members will bring pain to one another. When this happens, we can get angry and "throw in the towel," or we can recognize that the only healthy and God-pleasing solution is forgiveness. I found this definition of forgiveness: *"Forgiveness is a gift in which the injured one gives up the right to retaliate and is willing to restore a warm relationship."*

Greed and selfishness are the greatest enemies of marriage and the family. *"A greedy man brings trouble upon his family"* (Proverbs 15:27). Greed is wanting or taking all one can get without thought of what others need. It is a demand for self-gratification. With this selfish attitude, what I want becomes more important than my responsibility to my spouse or my children.

There are many ways we can increase the practice of love in our family living. I believe the most important is trusting the Holy Spirit to pour out God's love within our hearts. *"God has poured out his love into our hearts by the Holy Spirit, whom he has given us"* (Romans 5:5). To increase love (romantic, respect, and help), we need to let the love of God for us become more real and personal. As you grow closer to your Lord and experience His love more fully, it becomes much easier, and natural, to love your spouse, your children, and others as He loves you.

Feb 11

Chuckle: *"I've reached that age when a good day is one when I get up and nothing hurts."* ~ Satchel Paige

Quote: *"We are continually faced with a series of great opportunities brilliantly disguised as insoluble problems."* ~ John W. Gardner

Overwhelmed by Circumstances

"O God, listen to my cry! Hear my prayer! From the ends of the earth, I will cry to you for help, for my heart is overwhelmed. Lead me to the towering rock of safety" (Psalm 61:1-2 NLT).

Have you ever felt like you were at the end of your rope? That your life was totally out of control? That you wanted to "throw in the towel" and give up? When we feel overwhelmed, the important questions become: What do we do? How do we handle overwhelming circumstances? To whom do you turn when you are overcome with frustration, stress, fear, and pain?

Turn to God and claim His promises in these ways:

~ God's love: *"Nothing in all creation will ever be able to separate us from the love of God that is revealed in Christ Jesus our Lord"* (Romans 8:39 NLT). We can take solace in the fact that God's love is absolute, certain, consistent, and always with us to give us victory. When you feel overwhelmed, just "wallow" around in God's love, and trust Him to help you overcome whatever causes you to feel overwhelmed. "Blessed Assurance!"

~ God's presence: *"I am leaving you with a gift—peace of mind and heart. And the peace I give isn't like the peace the world gives"* (John 14:27 NLT). The gift of peace comes from the presence of the Holy Spirit. The Scriptures say we are the temple of the Holy Spirit—the dwelling place of the Spirit of Almighty God. Jesus said of the Holy Spirit, *"But you know him, for he lives with you and will be in you"* (John 14:17 NIV). This assurance, when contemplated, will give you deep and lasting peace of mind and heart.

~ God's Word: *"As pressure and stress bear down on me, I find joy in your commands"* (Psalm 119:143 NLT). God's Word is a source of deep, inexplicable joy and contentment, even during the most overwhelming of circumstances. *"Let the Word of Christ dwell in you richly . . . as you sing psalms, hymns, and spiritual songs with gratitude in your hearts to God"* (Colossians 3:16 NIV).

~ Prayer: *"Death had its hands around my throat; the terrors of the grave overtook me. I saw only trouble and sorrow. Then I called on the name of the Lord: 'Please, Lord, save me!'"* (Psalm 116:3-4 NLT). Praying includes talking to God honestly and listening as He speaks. Prayer will help you deal with the issues that may appear as overwhelming from a human perspective. But God's perspective is different.

Growing love relationship with God: *"Come to me, all of you who are weary and carry heavy burdens, and I will give you rest. Take my yoke upon you. Let me teach you, because I am humble and gentle, and you will find rest for your souls"* (Matthew 11:26-29 NLT). This relationship will help put difficult circumstances into perspective.

Feb 12

Chuckle: *"If I wanted to go crazy, I would do it in Washington because it would not be noticed."* ~ Irwin S. Cobb

Quote: *"Man is not at peace with his fellow man because he is not at peace with himself; he is not at peace with himself, because he is not at peace with God."* ~ Thomas Merton

Coping with Overwhelming Situations

"Give your burdens to the Lord, and he will take care of you. He will not permit the godly to slip and fall" (Psalm 55:22 NLT). *"Praise be to the Lord, to God our Savior, who daily bears our burdens"* (Psalm 68:19 NIV).

For the Christian, it's not how difficult life becomes, but how one handles and copes with those difficulties that makes the difference. One of the saddest experiences in my ministry is to see a "Christian" totally defeated and with no clue as to how to turn that defeat into victory. It seems seeking God in times of adversity is an alien concept to some.

Many try to figure things out and solve their problems in their own strength, instead of turning to the true source of strength and wisdom. They will try every possible solution, from the world's point of view, except drawing near to their God who specializes in overcoming impossible situations. The solution is to place complete trust and confidence in God at all times, but especially when you have reached the bottom of life's pit. *"I am overwhelmed, and you alone know the way I should turn"* (Psalm 142:3 NLT).

When you feel overwhelmed, remember to accept God's love, comfort, and mercy. His arms are long enough to reach even the most depressed and downtrodden. *"Don't be afraid,*

*for I am with you. Do not be dismayed, for I am your God. I will
strengthen you. I will help you. I will uphold you with my
victorious right hand"* (Isaiah 41:10 NLT).

This is a solemn promise God has made to His people—and
that includes you and me. You need not fear because (1) God is
always with you, (2) God has made it possible for Him to have a
relationship with you through Jesus Christ, and (3) God gives
you assurance of His strength, help, and victory over sin and
death. Are you aware of all the ways God helps you?

*"Why am I discouraged? Why so sad? I will put my hope in
God! I will praise him again—my Savior and my God"* (Psalm
42:5-6 NLT). There should never be hopelessness in the life of a
Christian—there is no such word in God's vocabulary. If you
are shedding tears of loneliness, depression, or hopelessness,
there is a solution. God is so good and He wants to restore the
joy of your salvation and give you a life of peace and happiness.
But you must turn to Him in every situation and allow Him to
have His way in your life.

Feb 13

Chuckle: *"I see our neighbors have returned our grill,"* the *wife commented. "They've had it for eight months, and I was afraid that in their move, they'd take it with them by mistake."*

"That was our grill?" shouted her husband. "I just paid twenty dollars for it at their yard sale!"

Quote: *"I say, the acknowledgement of God in Christ Accepted by thy reason, solves for thee all questions in the earth and out of it."* ~ Robert Browning

Lordship of Christ

"And now, just as you accepted Christ Jesus as your Lord, you must continue to live in obedience to him" (Colossians 2:6 NLT).

When you receive Jesus Christ into your heart and life as Savior, you have taken the first, but all important, step in a growing relationship with Him. The next step is to make Him Lord of your life and give Him dominion over everything you are and everything you do. To live in Him is to live with Him as Lord and the center of your life. Total surrender to His will is the only response that truly makes Him Lord.

When we make Christ our Lord, we will follow His leadership and allow Him to grow us into mature spiritual followers. He wants to be your daily companion to guide, direct, and teach you as you deal with the problems and challenges of life. When we decide to live for Him, we will make a total submission of our wills to Him. We will concentrate on learning more and more about Him and how we can live in Him more fully, depending upon the power of the Holy Spirit in all situations.

Calling Jesus Lord is one thing, but to live under His

Lordship daily is another matter entirely. Jesus is keenly aware when what we profess and what we practice do not match. Jesus addressed this question to His listeners, *"Why do you call me, 'Lord, Lord,' and do not do what I say?"* (Luke 6:46 NIV). Making Christ Lord of your life means obeying His commands. The term "Lord" is much more than a polite title of respect for Christ when speaking of our relationship with Him. The term Lord means Master and calls us to sacrificial living and strict obedience.

There are three ways a skier can get to the top of the ski slope. He can try to walk up on his own. He can be pulled up as he holds on to a strap. Or he can ride up in the chair lift. This illustration vividly depicts the various ways Christians try to live the victorious Christian life. Some try completely in their own strength. Others try to combine their own effort with some degree of dependence on God. But the only way to know true victory in every situation is total dependence on the Holy Spirit, and submission to the Lordship of Christ.

Would you join me in a new commitment to really make Christ our Lord, and in the power of the Spirit, endeavor each day to reflect that relationship? If we do this, He will grant us an extra measure of peace, joy, and contentment.

Feb 14

Chuckle: *"A man will laugh at a woman putting on makeup, and then take ten minutes trying to make three hairs on top of his head look like six."*

Quote: *"Today is a most unusual day, because we have never lived it before; we will never live it again; it is the only day we have."* ~ William Arthur Ward

Live One Day at a Time

"If it is the Lord's will, we will live and do this or that" (James 4:15 NIV).

A few years back Christie Lane had a hit recording, and a portion of the lyrics went something like this: *"One day at a time, sweet Jesus, that's all I'm asking from you. Help me today. Show me the way, one day at a time."*

The only time any of us have is today—time can't be saved and it can't be retrieved—it can only be savored. I've heard it said, "If you want to make God laugh, tell Him about your plans for tomorrow." Several scriptures attest to the value of living for today.

"This is the day the Lord has made; let us rejoice and be glad in it" (Psalm 118:24 NIV). *"Do not worry about tomorrow, for tomorrow will worry about itself"* (Matthew 6:34 NIV). *"Do not boast about tomorrow, for you do not know what a day may bring forth"* (Proverbs 27:1 NIV). *"Why, you do not even know what will happen tomorrow"* (James 4:14 NIV).

Some live in the past and dwell on mistakes and failures which are now history and cannot be changed. Others live in the future in a constant state of expectancy and dissatisfaction with their lives today. Either of these mind-sets can cause us to miss the blessings God has for us today.

Living one day at a time means keeping yourself responsive to simple things. For most of us, there are few big moments in life—only a plethora of small ones. Most of us never win the Pulitzer Prize, or the Nobel Prize, or an Oscar. But we're all eligible for life's small pleasures: a pat on the back, a hug, a 12-point buck in your sights, a big bass on your line, a full moon, a crackling fire, a good meal, a glorious sunset.

If our happiness is dependent upon major accomplishments and events, we won't be happy much of the time. If, however, our happiness depends on a good breakfast, flowers in the yard, a brisk walk, or a nap, we will have a lot of happiness. A good motto would be: "Learn from yesterday, hope for tomorrow, but live for today." Living one day at a time will help make your life be all it can be. When you kill time, it has no resurrection! Today is the only certain time we have to share the love of Christ with someone.

Feb 15

Chuckle: *"My husband and I divorced over religious differences. He thought he was God and I didn't!"*

Quote for today: *"To be blind is bad, but worse is to have eyes and not see."*

~ Helen Keller

A Good Eye

"Your eye is a lamp for your body. A pure (good) eye lets sunshine into your soul. But an evil (bad) eye shuts out the light and plunges you into darkness. If the light you think you have is really darkness, how deep that darkness will be" (Matthew 6:22-23 NLT).

Those in law enforcement often find that multiple witnesses to the same crime will see the event with differing perceptions of what went down and what the perpetrator looked like. In other words, our eyes can sometimes fool us into thinking we see one thing when, in reality, we should have seen something entirely different. In the spiritual realm, our spiritual eyes/vision must be trained by God's Word and Holy Spirit to see clearly the reality of what God wants of us and to see the world as God sees it.

In the same way that we can train our physical eyes to accurately transmit to our minds true reality, we must also allow God to train our spiritual eyes to discern spiritual truth. When we are able to see spiritual truth clearly and accurately, our whole being will be filled with the light that only the Light of the World can provide.

The Message translation of our passage reads like this:

"Your eyes are windows into your body. If you open your eyes wide in wonder and belief, your body fills up with light." The next verse says, *"If you live squinty-eyed in greed and distrust, your body is a dank cellar. If you pull the blinds on your windows, what a dark life you will have."*

Our spiritual eyes perceive incorrectly the things of God because of a lack of understanding or discernment. It's easy to jump to conclusions and discredit a spiritual truth because our impaired spiritual vision transmits to our hearts and minds an incorrect image of God, His love, and His truths.

I'm sure you have heard *"there is none so blind as those who won't see."* Our spiritual eyes determine if we see light or darkness. If we make up our minds about God's truth using our distrustful squinty eyes and lack of faith, we can miss the amazing message of Scripture. *"For God so loved the world that he gave his one and only son, that whoever believes in him shall not perish but have eternal life"* (John 3:16 NIV).

Many of those who are lost will "pull the blinds on their windows" and miss experiencing the light of God's love and the eternal joy of knowing Christ and trusting Him. But Christians can also miss the joy of a close personal daily fellowship with Christ because we will not surrender completely to Him and let His Spirit light our way and give us 20/20 spiritual vision.

Feb 16

Chuckle: *If athletes get athletes foot, what do astronauts get? Missile Toe.*

Quote: *"An hour before sunrise—in creative meditation— can miraculously enrich the soul. A minute during a sunrise—in receptive silence—can gloriously inspire the heart."*
~ William Arthur Ward

God in the Morning

"In the morning, O Lord, you hear my voice; in the morning I lay my requests before you and wait with expectation" (Psalm 5:3 NIV).

I'm a morning person and an early riser. Perhaps this is the result of my years in the Army, when every day started at zero dark thirty. Seriously, there is something peaceful and precious about spending some time with our Lord in the early morning—before our minds become cluttered with the problems and pressures of the day. Of course you can study God's Word and pray at any time, but starting the day with God will set the tone for how you react to everything else that happens during the day.

Please notice in our passage how the psalmist brought his requests to God in the morning, then waited patiently and expectantly for God to answer and grant his requests. Regular communication strengthens any relationship. This is true not only between human beings, but is even more important for our relationship with God. Regular time spent with God is essential for our spiritual growth and the joy that comes from a warm fellowship with Him.

We must, however, realize that communicating with God

involves much more than voicing our shopping lists of requests and desires. God wants to speak to us through His Word and Spirit as we study, meditate, and pray. What God may say to us during our quiet time with Him is far more important than what we may want to say to God. What He says to us can change our lives. It is important that we approach God to listen as well as to ask.

"I listen carefully (expectantly) to what God the LORD is saying, for he speaks peace to his people, his faithful ones" (Psalm 85:8 NLT).

If early morning quiet time doesn't work well for you, it's important that you set aside a regular time and place each day to study God's Word and pray. God's answers to your prayers will come in His own time, and you are wise to wait patiently with both anticipation and expectation for those answers. If you aren't listening carefully, you may miss God's answers.

"Little of the Word with little prayer is death to the spiritual life. Much of the Word with little prayer gives a sickly life. Much prayer with little of the Word gives an emotional life. But a full measure of both the Word and prayer each day gives a healthy and powerful life." ~ Andrew Murray

Feb 17

Chuckle: *"What I've learned from dogs: If someone's chewing you out, it helps to stare into space like it's not happening."* ~ Mark Patinkin

Quote: *"People are lonely because they build walls instead of bridges. Let us not erect walls without doors of friendliness or windows of love."* ~ Joseph Fort Newton

Overcoming Loneliness

"Turn to me and be gracious to me (O God), for I am lonely and afflicted. The troubles of my heart have multiplied. Free me from my anguish" (Psalm 25:16-17 NIV).

How many people are drowning in loneliness and despair all around us while no one notices, or worse, no one cares? Some struggle with the need for companionship and kindness, but often their cries go unheard. We assemble ourselves at church unaware that someone seated next to us is going under for the third time in a sea of loneliness.

Some think Christians are immune from loneliness and fear. There is an unspoken belief that genuine Christians don't have problems like that. We all know that's not true. We come to church and sing, "Rescue the Perishing," and fail to notice that there are people perishing right there in the pews. Someone may be dealing with severe grief over the loss of a loved one. Another may have been abandoned by someone deeply loved. Another may have a loved one thousands of miles away in harm's way.

In our modern culture, which idealizes independence and individuality, we have paid the price with a loss of friendships, closeness, and community, even among Christians. Self-sufficiency can be a source of pride, but the result is that we no longer belong to anyone. You may be lonely yourself and in need of encouragement, or you may know someone mired deep in loneliness and are wondering how you can help. How can you ease the pain if you are lonely and perhaps help others? Here are some thoughts:

~ Stay true to your beliefs and practice integrity. Don't give up on yourself or others. Do your best to live by the values of your Christian faith, staying tuned to the wisdom of God's Word and the guidance of the Holy Spirit. Make up your mind to see the best in others rather than the worst. Focus on the positive, never the negative.

~ Find meaningful, productive, and satisfying work to do. Idleness contributes to the feelings of loneliness and uselessness, but productive work will give you purpose, make you feel better about yourself, and help dispel loneliness. Use your God-given abilities for the good of others.

~ Forgive those who may have wronged you. Lingering unwillingness to forgive will only intensify loneliness. You may feel you have done nothing to deserve the mistreatment you may have received, and you may be right. But that doesn't diminish the release and freedom that can come from forgiving the one who hurt you.

~ Finally, take God at His Word when He says, *"Never will I leave you; never will I forsake you"* (Hebrews 13:5 NIV). Those who walk with God are never really alone. It is not what happens to us that matters, but how we handle what happens to us. God specializes in solving problems, and He will help you overcome loneliness if you allow Him to do so.

Feb 18

Chuckle: *A patient awakened after the operation to find herself in a room with all the blinds drawn. "Why are all the blinds closed?" she asked the doctor. "Well," the surgeon responded, "they're fighting a huge wildfire across the street, and we didn't want you to wake up and think the operation had failed."*

Good Quote: *"God created memories so that we might have roses in December."* ~ Italo Svevo

Precious Memories

"I remember your wonderful deeds of long ago. They are constantly in my thoughts. I cannot stop thinking about them" (Psalm 77:11-12 NLT).

When I conduct a funeral I usually remind the family that both their capacity to grieve the loss of a loved one and to remember the wonderful blessings of that life are gifts from God. Just stop and think about the intricacies of the human brain and spirit that make grieving and remembering possible—not to mention all the other amazing functions our brains perform. The more you think about these two capabilities, the more amazing and miraculous they become. They remind us of the omnipotence of our Heavenly Father who wonderfully created each of us and faithfully sustains us.

Right now, let's use our ability to remember and think about all the great things God has done for us and our families. Remember how God, because of His great love, came into your life with His miraculous plan of redemption through His Son's atoning sacrifice. Remember how He continues to work in your life through His Word and His powerful indwelling Holy Spirit.

Remember how He has arranged circumstances in your life that show how deeply He cares for you. Remember how He gave you your spouse, your children, your ability to work and earn a living, your sense of humor, your precious friends, your brothers and sisters in Christ, and everyone and everything of value to you.

Remember when His Word brought you peace and comfort during difficult times— how the presence of the Holy Spirit has brought you joy from knowing God is with you no matter what. When you face new and unexpected trials, take the time to remember, reflect, and review how His goodness has sustained you in the past. As you remember, your faith will be strengthened, your hope in Him will become absolute assurance, and your faithfulness to Him will be reaffirmed.

The chorus of the old hymn: *"Precious memories, How they linger; How they ever flood my soul. In the stillness of the midnight, Precious sacred scenes unfold."*

Let's thank God for the ability to remember and for the precious memories that bring great joy to our lives.

Feb 19

Chuckle: *The worst analogy ever written in a high school essay was . . . "Her hair glistened in the rain like a nose hair after a sneeze!"*

Good Quote: *"All that I have seen teaches me to trust the Creator for all I have not seen."* ~ Ralph Waldo Emerson

New Creation

"So we have stopped evaluating others by what the world thinks about them. Once I mistakenly thought of Christ that way, as though he were merely a human being. How differently I think about him now! What this means is that those who become Christians become new persons (new creations). They are not the same anymore, for the old life is gone. A new life has begun!" (2 Corinthians 5:16-17 NLT).

This passage contains one of the most miraculous truths in Scripture. When a person is saved by grace through faith in Jesus Christ, he or she becomes a new creation—a brand-new person on the inside. By the working of the Holy Spirit, he or she is not the same anymore. Rather, we think differently, speak differently, and act differently. We have a new nature. In the first creation, God brought people into physical existence from nothingness. In this new creation, He brings us from spiritual death to spiritual life.

Christians are not reformed, rehabilitated, or re-educated, but are transformed human beings living in an eternal union with Christ. This new relationship with Christ becomes the controlling factor in one's life. When we are converted/saved, it is not the equivalent of turning over a new leaf and promising to do better. It is the beginning of a new life under the control of a new Master. As a new creation in Christ, we receive a new nature with a new attitude toward God and life itself. We are no longer driven by the standards of the world, but by the standards of God's Word.

"For we are God's workmanship, created in Christ Jesus to do good works, which God prepared in advance for us to do" (Ephesians 2:10 NIV). The Message Bible puts it this way: *"He (God) creates each of us by Christ Jesus to join him in the work he does, the good work he has gotten ready for us to do, work we had better be doing."*

Notice that our salvation is not the result of doing good deeds. No, our salvation is by grace through faith—resulting in our re-creation. Then, as a natural progression from our rebirth, God expects us to do the work which He has arranged in advance for us to do. As a new creation, we do the work (ministry) of God while empowered by and under the direction of His Spirit. *"When God's work is done in God's way for God's glory, it will never lack God's supply. God is not obligated to pay for our selfish schemes. He is obligated to support his ministry."* ~ Hudson Taylor

Feb 20

Chuckle: *A child's answer to a science test question: "What does the word "benign' mean?" Answer: "It is what you will be after you be eight."*

Quote: *"What we have done for ourselves alone dies with us; what we have done for others and the world remains and is immortal."* ~ Albert Pike

Living Sacrifice

"Therefore, I urge you, brothers, in view of God's mercy, to offer your bodies as living sacrifices, holy and pleasing to God— this is your spiritual act of worship" (Romans 12:1 NIV).

I'm sure you remember the Old Testament story of Abraham and his son, Isaac, found in Genesis, chapter 22. The short version: God tested Abraham's faith by commanding him to sacrifice Isaac as a burnt offering. Abraham did as God commanded. He bound Isaac, laid him on the wood, and raised his knife to kill him. As he raised the knife, God stopped him and said to him: *"Now I know that you fear God, because you have not withheld from me your son, your only son"* (Genesis 22:12 NIV). God provided a ram to be offered instead of Isaac after Abraham had passed the test of faith. You see, God did not want Isaac to die. He had great plans for both Abraham and Isaac. He wanted both of them to be living sacrifices.

The message for us is that God wants us to love and trust Him so completely that we will sacrifice ourselves by dying to self and living lives of sacrifice for Him. He wants us to sacrifice through identification with Jesus' death which then makes it possible for us to live and do as Jesus did. Doing the will of our heavenly Father becomes our first priority.

Oswald Chambers puts it this way:

"I am willing to be identified with Your (Jesus') death so that I may sacrifice my life to God." He goes on to say: *It is of no value to God to give him your life for death. He wants you to be a living sacrifice, to let him have all your powers that have been saved and sanctified through Jesus. This is the thing (sacrifice) that is acceptable to God."*

Salvation is a free gift, which we do not deserve, made possible by God's love and grace through faith in Jesus Christ. It is not something we can earn. Because of God's free gift, we owe Him everything we have and are. We owe Him ourselves and all we have as an act of sacrificial worship. Our worship should be a matter of applying faith to everyday life. This is possible when God changes our mind-set by His Spirit working in us, giving us the ability to discern God's will in all we do.

Feb 21

Chuckle: *"Back in the sixties when the economy was suffering in England, some consideration was given to selling the Rock of Gibraltar to the French. All negotiations were halted when the British learned the French were planning to rename it "De Gaulle Stone."*

Good Quote: *"That best portion of a good man's life, His little, nameless, unremembered acts Of kindness and love."* ~ William Wordsworth

Making a Difference

"You obey the law of Christ when you offer each other a helping hand" (Gal. 6:2 CEV).

Sometimes you may feel like a total failure. You may perceive that your life is not positively impacting anyone in a meaningful way. You may think the routine of your day is unimportant. You may think that you should be doing more with the life God has given you. Welcome to the club. I suspect we have all had similar feelings.

Recently I received a kind note from one of my devotional readers who said a particular lesson had met a specific need at a critical time in his life. It's always good to know that our lives and ministries are having a positive impact. However, when such comments of affirmation and encouragement are not forthcoming, it's good to remember who we are serving and from whom our most important encouragement should come. As Christians, our service is to our Lord, and we serve Him by serving others—meeting the needs of people around us. It is His approval that should be our motivation, not the response of the people we serve.

A sign read *"There is no limit to the good that a man can do, if he doesn't care who gets the credit."* If you really don't care who gets the credit, then you can just enjoy yourself and do all kinds of good deeds for others. Just be glad that it is done, and don't worry about who gets the credit on earth, because your heavenly Father knows.

Just think of the lives you touch each day: family members, neighbors, workmates, classmates, etc. Consider those who depend on you. Think about the positives in your life. The great preacher, Dwight L. Moody once wrote: *"He does the most for God's great world who does the best in his own little world."* Jesus always encourages His followers to be faithful in the little things of life, as unimportant as they may seem to us.

You are God's unique creation, with unique gifts and abilities and you can make a difference. All around you there are people who need a hug, a pat on the back, a word of encouragement, a show of genuine love and compassion. Just love them as Jesus loves them. There's no better time than the present to refocus on touching the lives of others in kindness and love. A helping hand reveals the condition of the heart.

Feb 22

Chuckle: *A woman says to the postal clerk, "May I have 70 Christmas stamps?*

The clerk asks, "What denomination?"

The woman says, "Lord help us. Has it come to this? Give me 8 Catholic, 12 Episcopalian, 8 Methodist, 9 Presbyterian, 10 Lutheran and 22 Baptists."

Good Quote: *"The corn that makes the holy bread By which the soul of man is fed, The holy bread, the food unpriced, The everlasting mercy, Christ."* ~ John Masefield

The Miracle of Mercy

"He who covers (hides) his transgressions (sins) will not prosper, but whoever confesses and forsakes his sins will obtain mercy" (Proverbs 28:13 AMP).

Sin is not a favorite word in our modern vocabulary. We would much prefer to call our impure thoughts and actions by other terms such as mistakes, errors, or short-comings. But we are wise to deal honestly with the meaning of sin as it relates to the way we live. In the original language, the word "sin" means to miss the mark that God has set for us—to miss living by God's standards for human conduct—to rebel against God. The word "sin" describes those ungodly things we do, the good things we fail to do, and the condition into which everyone is born.

The greatest sin of all is rejecting God's free gift of salvation through faith in Jesus Christ. The wonderful truth is that our merciful God will forgive all our sins if we genuinely repent and ask His forgiveness and cleansing. We all need to be reminded that *"all have sinned and fall short of the glory of God"*

(Romans 3:23 NIV).

When you ignore your sins and try to conceal them, you do major harm to yourself and sometimes to others. Sins that are not dealt with create a lifestyle which includes many individual sins. A destructive cycle of rebelliousness and deception is created within you. In the same way Adam and Eve wanted to hide their sins from God, it is human nature to try to hide ours from Him and others. Something deep within us strongly resists admitting that we have sinned—done wrong. But when we openly and humbly admit our sins and seek God's forgiveness, a healing process begins that will ultimately result in a sense of well-being, peace, and eternal security.

Even though Christians have been saved from the eternal penalty for their sins, we all need to continually confess our sins to God, and admit that we need God's mercy and forgiveness each day we live. *"If we confess our sins, he is faithful and just and will forgive our sins and purify us from all unrighteousness"* (1 John 1:9 NIV). When we accept God's mercy, forgiveness, and cleansing, He sets us free from the damaging cycle of sin in our lives and also frees us from the anger, bitterness, rebelliousness, and corruption that precipitated our sinful actions.

We should fall on our faces before God in gratitude and praise Him for His love, mercy, and grace. Further, we should seek God's forgiveness for failing to ask for His mercy and forgiveness. Without the shed blood of Jesus and God's boundless love, amazing grace, and infinite mercy, there would be no forgiveness of sins.

Feb 23

Chuckle: *On a cold, snowy Sunday in February, only the pastor and one farmer arrived at the village church. The pastor said, "Well I guess we won't have a service today."*

The farmer replied, "If only one cow shows up at feeding time, I feed it."

Quote: *"Who will not mercy to others show, How can he mercy ever hope to have."* ~ Edmund Spenser

The Mission of Mercy

"Show mercy to those whose faith is wavering. Rescue others by snatching them from the flames of judgment. There are still others to whom you need to show mercy, but be careful that you aren't contaminated by their sins" (Jude 22-23 NLT).

Every Christian, without exception, has been dispatched by our Lord on a mission of mercy to claim or reclaim two categories of people: The lost who have never committed their lives to Jesus Christ. And those believers who have drifted away from God as their faith has become weakened. Our passage also contains a warning that we must be on guard against letting their sinful habits contaminate our own lives as we reach out to them.

Our assignment is to be faithful witnessing to others. Effective witnesses are instrumental in saving people from the penalty of their sins. Such witnessing requires unconditional love, mercy, compassion, patience and perseverance. We are God's messengers whom He uses to draw people to Himself for salvation and spiritual revival. There are numerous ways you can be an effective witness. A 12th century monk named Francis of Assisi (Italian) said, *"Preach everywhere you go and, when necessary, use words."*

Our actions, the company we keep, our faithfulness to Christ's church, and the words we utter are all important for effective witness. Have you ever pictured yourself extending the hand of love to snatch someone from the very perils of hell? If we don't snatch them, they are doomed for all of eternity. When I think of snatching someone from the fires of judgment, I'm reminded of the times I've cooked hamburgers on a grill and had one of the patties fall through the grill into the coals below. My first reaction is to snatch it out before it burns and without getting burned myself.

Notice the warning! As we witness, we must not become contaminated by the sins of those we are trying to reach. We must be careful not to fall into the quicksand of compromise. We must not allow them to influence us to sin. We do this by insuring that our own spiritual footing remains solid and secure.

Our passage is a clarion call to action for God's people. We are on a critical mission of mercy to rescue those around us from spending eternity separated from God in a place the Bible calls hell. We are to love wayward Christians back into a renewed and dynamic love relationship with Jesus Christ. *"Two works of mercy set a man free; forgive and you will be forgiven, and give and you will receive."* ~ St Augustine of Hippo, *Sermons*

Feb 24

Chuckle: *Sign in a small cafe with great food and an attitude: "If you can't smell it, we ain't got it!"*

Great Quote: *"Your light is the truth of the Gospel message itself as well as your witness as to who Jesus is and what He has done for you. Don't hide it."* ~ Anne Graham Lotz

One Little Candle

"Don't hide your light under a basket! Instead, put it on a stand and let it shine for all. In the same way, let your good deeds shine out for all to see, so that everyone will praise your heavenly Father" (Matthew 5:15-16 NLT).

During the last general election I'm sure many decided that "my one vote won't make any difference, so why bother." If you allowed this kind of logic to rob you of the privilege and satisfaction of exercising one of our most precious rights as citizens, I hope you will reconsider next time. If the millions of Americans had voted who did not vote, the outcome might have been different in many races. A single vote does make a difference.

Sadly, I think many Christians have a similar attitude about the importance of their testimony and witness for Christ. It's easy to say, "I'm just one little insignificant candle and the light of my witness won't make much difference in this world of darkness. I think this is one of Satan's most insidious tactics— to make you think you are useless to God so why even try to serve Him.

The great evangelist, Dwight L. Moody said, *"Remember, a small light will do a great deal when it is in a very dark place. Put one little tallow candle in the middle of a large hall, and it will give a great deal of light."*

Jesus is the Light of the world, and it is our duty to let His light be reflected through us by our words and actions that honor Him and communicate His love to others. I'm reminded of an old hymn that goes like this:

> *While passing thro' this world of sin, And others your life shall view, Be clean and pure without, within, Let others see Jesus in you. Keep telling the story, Be faithful and true, Let others see Jesus in you.*

During a recent Christmas candlelight service I was reminded that the light of individual Christians can have a significant impact on those around them. But when the lights of all Christians are shining in unison, great areas of darkness can be bathed in the light of Christ's love. Please don't ever underestimate your importance as a single candle in Christ's "Light Brigade!" I heard someone say, *"It's far better to light a single candle than to curse the darkness."*

Feb 25

Chuckle: *Carrying three pieces of luggage, a young woman approached the airport check-in counter and said, "I want this first piece of luggage sent to Cleveland, the second to Toronto, and the third to Miami."*

The agent said, "I'm sorry, we can't do that."

The young lady replied, "You did it last month."

Quote: *"Drop Thy still dews of quietness, Till all our strivings cease; Take from our souls the strain and stress, And let our ordered lives confess The beauty of Thy peace."*
~ John Greenleaf Whittier

Peace for the Storms

"I am leaving you with a gift—peace of mind and heart. And the peace I give isn't like the peace the world gives. So don't be troubled or afraid" (John 14:27 NLT).

Is there anxiety, worry, stress, or fear of the unknown in your life? When you go to bed at night, do you lie awake fretting and stewing about things over which you have little or no control? If you answered "yes" to these questions, you have joined a club with a multitude of members. Many depend upon tranquilizers and other mind-altering medications to relieve their anxieties and give them a sense of peace. For those of us who are Christians, there is a wonderful non-chemical solution for our lack of peace—the gift Jesus wants us to receive.

In our passage, Jesus was about to leave the disciples and be crucified. But He did not want to leave them without presenting them a special gift—His peace. This gift is real and can be possessed by every believer. The world may wish you peace, but it cannot give it as Jesus can. This peace is a confident assurance that God is in control in every situation. With this peace, we have no need to fear anything in the present or in the future. Christ's peace *". . . which transcends all understanding, will guard your hearts and your minds"* (Philippians 4:7b NIV).

The peace that Jesus gives is not troubled by storms in our lives; and neither is it intimidated by challenges we must face. We need not be afraid, but we do need to be faithful in our walk with our Lord. You may ask, "How do I get from the head knowledge that Jesus grants me peace to a heart that actually experiences this peace?"

His presence within us (Holy Spirit) is the source of peace that only Christ Jesus can give. The promise of His peace is connected to the promise of the Holy Spirit to indwell us. Love, joy, and *peace* are among the fruits of the Spirit (Galatians 5:22). We must depend upon the promise from our Lord and accept this gift in faith and gratitude while turning all our worries, fears, and anxieties over to Him. I'm reminded of this line from an old hymn: "Take your burdens to the Lord and leave them there."

Feb 26

Chuckle: *"How long have you been driving without a tail light,"* the policeman asked the lady he had pulled over.

"Oh, no!" the woman screamed as she ran to the back of the car.

"Just calm down," said the officer. "It's not that serious."

"But it's my husband I'm worried about. He's in the trailer that was hitched to the car!"

Quote: *"Life is too short to be small."* ~ Disraeli

Pettiness

"A man's wisdom gives him patience; it is to his glory to overlook an offense" (Proverbs 19:11 NIV).

Petty means "of little importance; small; minor; trivial. Narrow minded or ungenerous, especially in trifling matters. Of lesser importance or rank; subordinate. Having or showing a narrow, mean character." On the practical side, pettiness is like making mountains out of mole hills. We let small, unimportant, and insignificant things upset us and turn us into monsters that others do not want to be around.

Life is too short to worry and fret about the small stuff. The challenge for us is how to tell the small stuff from the really important stuff. All too often the small and insignificant becomes the elephant in the room in our minds. Do you have a short fuse when it comes to your pet peeves? We tend to want people to act right, follow the rules, and not do anything to hurt our feelings. I have seen "Christians" get their feelings hurt over some insignificant petty issue and either leave the church pouting like a child who didn't get his way, or carry a lasting grudge that disrupts the warm loving fellowship God wants for

His people.

Our passage says we should not be offended or personally affronted by the actions and choices of others. We are to be forgiving even when the offense is against us and even though it is difficult—even when we are hurt deeply by someone's words or deeds. It is God's responsibility to deal with the sinful actions of others, not ours. We are to love and forgive as God has loved and forgiven us.

I believe pettiness among Christians can be attributed to a lack of spiritual maturity. We should strive to become mature followers of Christ. In his New Testament writings, Paul describes his dealing with believers who were not maturing and pettiness was often the result, especially in new congregations. Here's what Paul said to the Corinthians, *"When I was a child I talked like a child, I thought like a child, I reasoned like a child. When I became a man I put childish ways behind me"* (1 Corinthians 13:11 NIV). As we mature spiritually, we become more and more like Jesus. Selfishness and pettiness are replaced by love, compassion, patience, and forgiveness.

"Every day, God grants us the precious gift of life. Yet every day, we squander it with our selfish, petty concerns, rather than helping someone as He helps us." ~ Kirn Hans, *Behind My Mask*

Feb 27

Chuckle: *"Encouragement is like a peanut butter sandwich—the more you spread it around, the better things stick together."*

Quote: *"If you think that praise is due him, Now is the time to slip it to him, For he cannot read his tombstone when he's dead."* ~ Berton Braley

Praising Others

"Let another praise you, and not your own mouth; someone else, and not your own lips" (Proverbs 27:2 NIV).

Praise, compliments, commendations, affirmations, and other words of encouragement are welcomed and appreciated by all of us. Words like great job—I'm proud of you—I believe in you— can inspire, invigorate, and change lives. Of course, our primary motive for Christian service should be to please and glorify our Lord and merit His approval. *"For it is not the one who commends himself who is approved, but the one whom the Lord commends"* (2 Corinthians 10:18 NIV).

However, we all enjoy having others commend us for what we do. When someone praises us, it brings feelings of self-worth and confidence. Such praise provides an additional motivation for even greater faithfulness in our service to God and other people. Encouraging one another is a major theme in the New Testament, and praise is a great means of encouragement.

I ran across an old England saying, *"Just praise is a debt to be paid."* In other words, we owe it to others to praise them when such praise is truly merited. However, praise that is not merited will cause the recipient of such praise to lose confidence in us because he or she knows we aren't being truthful. Conversely, praise that is merited but not expressed also discredits our character. Withholding legitimate praise can be the result of envy or resentment because we believe merited praise is being withheld from us. Obviously, this should not be the attitude of a loving, caring Christian. We should praise others without expecting praise for ourselves. However, kindness has a way of returning to us in even greater measure than that which we have extended.

Sometimes lasting and treasured friendships are born out of expressions of praise. If we know someone believes in us, appreciates what we have done, and tells us so, we are drawn to that person in a powerful and unique way. A thoughtful person who praises you will serve as a role-model for you in your relationships with others. The simple courtesy of "thank you for enriching my life with your kindness and faithfulness" can bring cheer to someone who knew they deserved praise but never considered the possibility that they would receive it.

Finally, it is much better if we seek the praise of God rather than the praise of people. Then, when we receive praise from people, we will be free and willing to give God the credit.

Feb 28

Chuckle: *Sunday school teacher: "Children, you must never do anything in private you wouldn't do in public."*

"Hurrah!" shouted one little boy—"No more baths!"

Quote: *"The race is not always to the swift but to those who keep on running."* ~ Unknown

Race for the Crown

"I have fought the good fight, I have finished the race, I have kept the faith. Now there is in store for me the crown of righteousness, which the Lord, the righteous Judge, will award to me on that day . . . ." (2 Timothy 4:7-8 NIV).

If you have watched the Olympics on television, you have no doubt seen the expressions on the faces of the runners as they strain to reach the finish line. The television cameras make it possible for us to see every detail of the race. Looking into the runner's faces, we see athletes straining every muscle, every sinew, and every ligament as they approach the finish line. We see the blood vessels bulging in their necks and across their brows. Each is giving it all he or she has, keeping nothing in reserve, and leaving nothing in the tank. The one goal is to win the race and he or she will settle for nothing less than victory.

The apostle Paul often used athletic analogies to drive home spiritual truths. He saw his faithful service to his Lord as a race to be all God wanted him to be. No athlete I've known was ever successful without giving his all in training for running and finishing the race. Winning athletes don't settle for mediocrity. Their goal is not to work just hard enough to get by. They give their all.

Paul painted this word picture for us, *"Do you not know that in a race all the runners run, but only one gets the prize?" Run in such a way as to get the prize. Everyone who competes in the games goes into strict training. They do it to get a crown that will not last; but we do it to get a crown that will last forever"* (1 Corinthians 9:24-25 NIV).

What is the goal Paul is straining to attain at the end of his race? Very simply, it is to be faithful to his goal of becoming like Jesus. His aim was to exert every possible effort and ounce of energy to accomplish his goal. God deserves nothing less than our very best in everything we do for his glory. Like the athlete who gives all he has to win, God expects us to give all we have to grow and become more mature Christians. If we have the "want to," God's Word will teach us the "how to," and His Holy Spirit will give us the "can do" to successfully run, finish, and win the race set before us.

Today is a great time to examine our hearts to determine how much we want to please our Lord. How much time and energy are we willing to expend for Christ when compared to the energy we expend on other things? Are we depending upon His Spirit to give us strength to finish the race God has called us to run? Now is a great time to make a new commitment to spiritual growth and faithfulness.

Feb 29

Chuckle: *Sign on plumber's truck: "We repair what your husband fixed!"*

Quote: *"Science may have found a cure for most evils, but is has found no remedy for the worst of them all—the apathy of human beings."* ~ Helen Keller

Apathy, A Moral and Spiritual Cancer

"Now this was the sin of your sister Sodom: She and her daughters were arrogant, overfed and unconcerned (apathetic); they did not help the poor and needy. They were haughty and did detestable things before me. Therefore I did away with (destroyed) them as you have seen" (Ezekiel 16:49-50 NIV).

Someone was asked if he knew the difference between ignorance and apathy. His reply, "I don't know and I don't care." I'm afraid this describes the attitude of many of us both spiritually and socially. The dictionary defines apathy as *"A lack of interest or concern; indifference."* For example, public *apathy* resulted in a light voter turnout.

When elections come around, a large segment of the adult population will not care enough to even cast a ballot. But sadly, many of those same apathetic Americans will gripe and complain if people they don't like are voted into office and make political decisions contrary to their values.

I pray you are neither disinterested nor unconcerned when it comes to exercising your constitutional right and precious freedom to make your voice heard at the ballot box. Please care enough to cast your all-important vote for those candidates who best exemplify the moral and spiritual standards set forth in God's Word. Your vote could make the difference in a close election.

Sadly, apathy is not limited to the political process. It is also alive and well in the spiritual realm among many who call themselves Christians. It is God's will that His people be actively involved in evangelizing and ministering to the spiritual, physical, and emotional needs of people. God is not interested in our offerings, ceremonies and celebrations if we are apathetic about the plight of those around us.

God said, *"Learn to do right! Seek justice, encourage the oppressed, plead the case of the widow"* (Isaiah 1:17 NIV). *"I hate, I despise your religious feasts; I cannot stand your assemblies . . . Away with the noise of your songs! I will not listen to the music of your harps. But let justice roll on like a river, righteousness like a never-failing stream!"* (Amos 5:21, 23-24 NIV).

Jesus is concerned about the apathy of His followers as workers in His harvest fields. When He saw the crowds, He had compassion on them, because they were harassed and helpless, like sheep without a shepherd. Then He said to His disciples, *"The harvest is plentiful but the workers are few. Ask the Lord of the harvest, therefore, to send workers into his harvest field"* (Matthew 9:36-38 NIV).

Let's pray. Lord, please rearrange my heart, mind, and will to make me intolerant of the sin of apathy both in my relationship with you and in carrying out my civic and social responsibilities. In Jesus' name, Amen.

Mar 01

Chuckle: *"A little boy kept looking at the rack of greeting cards. The clerk asked if she could help him—Birthday? Illness? Wedding?*

The boy shook his head no and answered wistfully, "Got anything in the line of blank report cards?"

Quote: *"Be not miserable about what may happen tomorrow. The same everlasting Father, who cares for you today, will care for you tomorrow." ~* Francis deSales

God and the Broken-Hearted

"The Lord is close to the broken-hearted; he rescues those who are crushed in spirit" (Psalm 34:18 NLT). *"He heals the broken-hearted, binding up their wounds"* (Psalm 147:3 NLT).

Wouldn't it be wonderful if we could escape the pain of grief, loss, disappointment, sorrow, and failure? But troubles are a part of life and come to all of us. God does not promise us trouble-free lives, but He does promise to be "close to the broken-hearted" and to be our source of strength, courage, and wisdom as He helps us to deal with our heartaches.

One of the most severe by-products of a broken heart is the deep sense of loneliness. When our hearts have been broken, everyone and everything around us can become distant, out of focus, and of limited value in helping us deal with the situation. On the other hand, if we turn to Him, God not only has the answers for mending a broken heart, but He will actively participate in its healing. God makes some amazing promises to the broken-hearted.

Let's face it, the Christian life is not always easy. Broken hearts and disappointments are commonplace. They may be the result of an unfaithful spouse, a rebellious child, betrayal by a trusted friend, or the result our own indiscretions and bad choices. There are times when everything is out of whack and nothing makes sense—the whole world seems to be crumbling around you.

From our passage, we see that God not only understands, but is always near to the broken-hearted and wants to heal the wounds responsible for our sorrow. He will comfort the broken-hearted by His presence, compassion, listening ear, abiding love, healing hand, encouragement, and blessings. When one of His children is broken-hearted, so is our Lord.

So how should I react to a broken heart? When heart-breaking experiences come your way, don't get frustrated with God. Instead, admit that you need God's help and thank Him for being by your side. Call to Him in your time of need and be honest with your feelings. He loves you and will draw you close by His presence.

"Come quickly, Lord, and answer me, for my depression deepens. Don't turn away from me, or I will die. Let me hear of your unfailing love to me in the morning, for I am trusting you. Show me where to walk, for I have come to you in prayer" (Psalm 143:7-8 NLT).

Chuckle: A child's comment on the Bible: *"The epistles were the wives of the apostles."*

Quote: *"There is no despair so absolute as that which comes with the first moments of our great sorrow, when we have not yet known what it is to have suffered and be healed, to have despaired and recovered hope."* ~ George Eliot

Helping the Broken-hearted

"He comforts us in all our troubles so that we can comfort others. When others are troubled, we will be able to give them the same comfort God has given us" (2 Corinthians 1:4 NLT). *"When others are happy, be happy with them. If they are sad, share their sorrow"* (Romans 12:15 NLT).

The dictionary defines "broken-hearted" as "Full of sorrow or despair; very unhappy." When our hearts are broken, it's difficult to think of anyone but ourselves. We are hurting so badly that the plight of others is sometimes obscured by our own pain. But, in my spiritual journey, I have been greatly inspired by godly people who had the strength to be more concerned for others than themselves even in the most heart-breaking circumstances. When we see someone like that, it indicates a level of faith and trust in our Lord that should be the goal of each of us. Even when your heart is breaking, God can use you to help comfort others. Your troubles can give you great understanding and insight into the feelings of others whose hearts are likewise broken.

Once you have taken your broken heart to the Lord and He has given you His peace, comfort, and strength, He definitely wants to use you as a blessing to others. You can encourage others who are broken-hearted by your presence, and with words of comfort—words that will lift up the hurting. God will give you the ability to remain strong and steadfast in your own faith so that the weakened and discouraged will seek your counsel as someone who has gained credibility by overcoming a similar hurt.

"We have been greatly comforted, dear brothers and sisters, in all of our own crushing troubles and suffering, because you have remained strong in your faith" (1 Thessalonians 3:7 NLT).

God can heal your brokenness. And His healing will give you an inner peace and cause you to rejoice. As others see God's healing in your life, and your rejoicing, they will rejoice with you. There will never be a time in your Christian life when God cannot use you to bless others if only you can get outside yourself and see those around you who are hurting.

"Faith, like light, should always be simple and unbending; while love, like warmth, should beam forth on every side, and bend to every necessity of our brothers and sisters."
~ Martin Luther

Mar 03

Chuckle: *A woman remarked to a man at a party, "You know . . . you look like my third husband."*

"How many times have you been married?" asked the man.

"Twice," replied the lady!"

Quote: *"Unless we place our religion and our treasure in the same thing, religion will always be sacrificed." ~* Epictetus

Trinkets or Treasures

"Don't store up treasures here on earth, where they can be eaten by moths and get rusty, and where thieves break in and steal. Store your treasures in heaven, where they will never become moth-eaten or rusty and where they will be safe from thieves. Wherever your treasure is, there your heart and thoughts will also be" (Matthew 6:19-21 NLT).

As a child, I enjoyed watching the old western movies. I remember how the settlers moving west would try to trade worthless trinkets to the Native Americans for things of much greater value like land, horses, food, etc. The Indians were intrigued by the uniqueness of things they had never seen and were confused about their real value. Today, I believe many people are confused about the difference between trinkets and treasures. All the glitzy, enticing, and empty things valued by the world can easily confuse even Christians as to what is really important in life.

Jesus was aware that material needs are a reality to all people. He took those needs very seriously and had much to say about them. Material things are not bad in and of themselves. They become bad when they become more important than our relationship with God. Jesus said, *"But seek first his (God's) kingdom and his righteousness and all these (material) things will be given to you as well"* (Matthew 6:33 NIV).

Here Jesus is teaching us that the most valuable treasure is found as we become Christians and focus our energy and attention on the things of His kingdom—things important to God. Everything else is worthless in comparison. However, notice Jesus' promise to provide for our physical needs when we place God first in our lives.

As Jesus taught His followers in the Sermon on the Mount (see Matthew, chapters 5 – 7), one of His major objectives was to teach us the difference between worthless trinkets and real treasures that will endure. Things of this world, regardless of their attractiveness, are mere worthless trinkets when compared with the eternal spiritual truths of God. No matter how much wealth we accumulate or how many possessions we have, they are utterly worthless compared to knowing Christ as Savior and Lord. In God's grand scheme of things, only our relationships with Him through faith in Jesus Christ will be of eternal value.

Once we know Christ as Savior, He expects us to begin storing up treasures in heaven by our acts of love and kindness. We seek to please God by our living, giving, and fulfilling His purpose for our lives. As you mature as a Christian, the Holy Spirit will give you the ability to discern what is a worthless trinket and what is a priceless treasure.

Mar 04

Chuckle: *Anger Management: A husband asks his wife, "When I get mad at you, you never fight back. How do you control your anger"?*

"I clean the toilet bowl."

"How does that help"?

"I use your toothbrush."

Good Quote: *"As we learn to shorten the time between offense and forgiveness, there becomes no time left for anger or vindictiveness."* ~ Unknown Source

Be Slow to Become Angry

"My dear brothers, take note of this: Everyone should be quick to listen, slow to speak and slow to become angry, for man's anger does not bring about the righteous life that God desires" (James 1:19-20 NIV).

We live in a time when a disagreement often becomes justification for personal attack, abuse, and sometimes even violence against the person or persons with whom we disagree. The ability to have civil and courteous discussions of divergent points of view seems to have been lost by many of us. It seems we have come to think a disagreement automatically means a fight. However, we must remember that anytime two or more people interact there will be disagreements from time to time.

Amicably discussing differing points can broaden our thinking on the issues and increase our appreciation and understanding of others. When we close our minds to points of view other than our own, we stop learning and increasingly expend our energies defending our own crystallized opinions.

Then our intolerance of other views continues to grow, and eventually that intolerance transfers from the issues to those expressing opposing views—it becomes personal. If not dealt with, the intolerance then festers within us and eventually gives way to full-blown hostility, anger, and even rage. Once this stage is reached, we may not stop talking but communications with those who disagree with us will stop, leaving no basis, or will, to better understand one another.

In our passage, we are admonished to be quick to listen. This means we accept everyone's right to speak and pay them respect by listening to them attentively. It does not mean we should necessarily abandon our convictions and adopt theirs. Rather, it means we recognize the right of others to have differing views. When we listen with patience, attentiveness, and courtesy, our attitude will not be lost on the one who is speaking. It takes two angry people to have a fight. As long as one person refuses to become angry, the possibility of mutual understanding increases—and good will is fostered.

Anger can become destructive and keep us from becoming the righteous person God wants us to be. I believe the first step in controlling our selfish anger is to pray for God's help. Then focus on seeing other people as God sees them—as precious souls who need the same love and forgiveness that we have received. It is impossible to remain angry with a person for whom you are sincerely praying. Finally, you might try to better understand the person instead of becoming angry. Once you understand his or her background and the challenges they face in life, you can better understand what makes them act the way they do.

Chuckle: *Geography teacher: "Who can describe the English Channel?"*

Student: "We don't get that channel on our TV."

Quote: *"A healthy (pure) conscience tugs at the concealed sin in our lives as though it were God's hidden hand."* ~ Unknown source

Deeply Troubled

"While Paul waited for them in Athens, he was deeply troubled by all the idols he saw everywhere in the city" (Acts 17:16 NLT).

We live in a society deeply engrossed in political correctness and tolerance of any and all lifestyles and immoral behavior. Is your spirit troubled by what you see? Tolerance is a good thing up to a point, but when it leads to complacency about things that are clearly wrong according to God's Word, even tolerance can become a sin.

Jesus tells us we are to be "salt and light" in an evil world—that we are to be an influence for that which is good, pure, holy, and true. The path of least resistance is to set back and let the world go by without lifting a finger or a voice against the corruption that permeates our communities and our nation. Are you deeply troubled by the deterioration in moral standards in your family, your community and your nation?

In our passage, the apostle Paul was deeply troubled by the idolatry and sinful living by the people of Athens. The Athenians were tolerant of any and all idolatry and conduct among the people. Paul was troubled to the point that he had to confront the Christian Jews and God-fearing Greeks. We should do as Paul did—look around us at the idols and be moved to do our part to represent Christ in our homes, schools, communities, clubs, workplaces, etc. If not now, when? If not you, who? Today's idols may be money, power, success, popularity, or false religions. Is our nation any different than Athens?

The gradual drift toward unbridled tolerance for sin can be traced to moral decay and sinful practices in our own lives. We can fill our minds with immoral images from television, movies, video games, and other media; and slowly and subtly we begin to compromise our moral standards. We become less and less offended by what we see. Then we not only tolerate those sinful images, but come to enjoy them. Our spiritual senses become dulled, our holiness is compromised, and we become useless to God as His ambassadors and messengers.

If we as God's people are to influence our society for good—integrity, morality, and holiness—we must begin with our own hearts and lives. We need pure consciences and godly actions. We should not blend in with the rest of a corrupt society. Instead, we should be a positive influence by following the example of Jesus who hates sin while loving the sinner.

Chuckle: *"Everybody's got it all wrong. Angels don't wear halos anymore. I forget why, but scientists are working on it."* ~ Olive, age 9

Ponder this: *"I expect to pass through this world but once; any good thing therefore that I can do, or any kindness that I can show to any fellow-creature, let me do it now; let me not defer or neglect it, for I shall not pass this way again."* ~ John Wesley

Kindness toward Others

"Get rid of all bitterness, rage, anger, harsh words, and slander, as well as all types of malicious behavior. Instead, be kind to each other, tender-hearted, forgiving one another, just as God through Christ has forgiven you" (Ephesians 4:31-32 NLT).

Paul's letter to the Ephesians describes the type behavior that ought to characterize the lives of Christians as we relate to one another. Our actions should be based on kindness and concern for others. Kindness has been defined as love expressed in practical ways. Love will make us more concerned with the needs of others than for our own. It should be our purpose to consider ways to meet other people's needs.

Being tender-hearted means that we are sensitive to how others feel. *"If one part (brother or sister) suffers, every part suffers with it; if one part is honored, every part rejoices with it"* (1 Corinthians 12:26 NIV). We grieve along with our brothers and sisters when they grieve. We also experience great joy when others are rejoicing. Being tender-hearted is showing empathy and compassion toward those around us.

We show forgiveness because we fall short of God's ideal and often need forgiveness ourselves. When we consider that

God has so graciously saved us from sin and destruction, we are motivated to forgive others when they offend us. Often we are less patient with our fellow Christians than with nonbelievers. Our expectations are higher for Christians, and sometimes we feel betrayed when they fail us. However, when we are tempted to be unforgiving, we need to look closely at the cross and remember the forgiveness we received there. God would have us set aside our self-centered attitude that causes us to be impatient and critical of others.

Jesus said the world will know we belong to Him by the love that we show to one another (see John 13:35). Are you often in conflict with others? If so, ask God to give you an extra measure of kindness, a tender heart, and a forgiving spirit. When you permit the Spirit to cultivate these qualities in you, your life will be a tremendous blessing to those around you. One of the most difficult things to give away is kindness, for it is usually returned! Have a great day as you show kindness to those around you!

Mar 07

Chuckle: *Patient: "Help me, Doc. I can't remember anything for more than a few minutes. It's driving me crazy!"*
Doctor: "How long has this been going on?"
Patient: "How long has what been going on?"
Quote: *"Kindness has converted more sinners than zeal, eloquence and learning."* ~ Robert Burns, *'A Winter Night'*

Kindness, Requested or Not

"Now swear to me by the LORD that you will be kind to me and my family since I have helped you" (Joshua 2:12 NLT).

Everyone desires to experience kindness. When someone shows an act of kindness to us, it makes us feel loved and accepted. It tells us we have value in the eyes of the one offering the kindness and encourages us to make similar gestures to others who may need of our kindness and compassion.

The words in our passage were spoken by Rahab, the prostitute, who had hidden the spies sent by Joshua to gather strategic information about the Promised Land, especially about the city of Jericho, in preparation for the upcoming battle. She had risked her life to give shelter to the Israelite spies in her house, which was likely built into the city wall. God directed the spies to Rahab's house because He knew her heart was receptive to Him and that she could provide the key to a successful siege of Jericho. Even her sordid past did not prevent God from using her to accomplish His purpose.

Rahab was aware that as the warriors of the Israelite army advanced across the Promised Land, their reputation preceded them and it was well known that the one and only true God was with them and helped them conquer every foe. In return for her help, Rahab asked only for kindness, not for herself alone but for her entire family. I'm sure the two spies understood the dangers facing Rahab if her king found out that she was aiding and abetting the enemy. *"We offer our own lives as a guarantee for your safety," the men agreed. "If you don't betray us, we will keep our promise when the LORD gives us the land"* (Joshua 2:14 NLT).

Rahab's request for kindness came because she saw something special and good in the spies. Do people see in your life the evidence of the God you serve? Is God's power revealed in you to the extent that people realize the authenticity of your faith and are drawn to you? If so, more than likely they will seek your kindness with questions about God. How open are you to the need to show kindness even if it is not requested? God shows kindness toward us because He loves us. Shouldn't we show kindness to others for the same reason—because we love them?

The greatest kindness you can offer anyone is to share your testimony about God's great love and what He has done for you. Your act of kindness can be used by the Holy Spirit to draw people into God's kingdom through their faith in Jesus Christ.

Chuckle: *Little Amy confided to her uncle, "When I grow up, I'm going to marry the boy next door."*

"Why is that?"

"'Cause I'm not allowed to cross the street."

Good Quote: *"Half an hour's listening is essential except when you are very busy. Then a full hour is needed."*
~ St Frances de Sales

Listen Very Carefully

"So we must <u>listen very carefully</u> to the truth we have heard, or we may drift away from it" (Hebrews 2:1 NLT).

I remember a game we played in my youth group when I was a teenager. It went like this: A person at the beginning of a long line of players would whisper something into the ear of the next person. That person then whispered what he had heard to the next person, and so it went to the end of the line. Then the last person would voice what he had heard and it was compared to what the first person had actually said. It was amazing, and sometimes hilarious, how distorted the original words could become. The distortion occurred from misunderstanding, embellishment, or just a failure to listen carefully.

Listen to what God said to His people through Moses, *"Moses called all the people of Israel together and said, 'Listen carefully to all the laws and regulations I am giving you today. Learn them and be sure to obey them!'"* (Deuteronomy 5:1 NLT).

In both our passages, a major emphasis is given to listening carefully to God, learning from God's words, and obeying what we have heard and learned. How carefully have you tuned your spiritual ears to listening to what God is saying to you? How committed are you to following God's directions so they do not become distorted, diluted, or irrelevant in your life because of the world's distractions?

James reminds us that listening carefully to the Word is the first step in becoming what God wants us to be. *"Do not merely listen to the word, and so deceive yourselves. Do what it says"* (James 1:22 NIV). We are to pay close attention and listen in a way that produces clear understanding with the intent to live out the instructions we have heard. Paying close attention involves focusing our minds, bodies, and senses. This will help insure that God's Word does not become distorted or forgotten in our daily lives. The ability to listen carefully to God and other people is a wonderful trait. The following is from an unknown source.

"His thoughts were slow,
His words were few and never formed to glisten.
But he was a joy to all his friends,
You should have heard him listen!"

Mar 09

Chuckle: *"These days, I spend a lot of time thinking about the hereafter. I go somewhere to get something and then wonder what I'm here after."*

Quote: *"The beginning of wisdom is silence. The second step is listening."* ~ Unknown Source

Be Quick to Listen

"My dear brothers, take note of this: Everyone should <u>be quick to listen</u>, slow to speak and slow to become angry, for man's anger does not bring about the righteous life that God desires" (James 1:19-20 NIV).

Although the two words are often used interchangeably, there is a great deal of difference between hearing and listening. The dictionary defines hearing as *"the act of receiving sound through the ears."* To listen is *"to pay attention to someone in order to hear."* As I recall from my physiology classes, hearing is the involuntary function of turning sound waves into electrical impulses which are received and interpreted in our brains. .

Listening, on the other hand, implies intent and effort—to pay attention. To listen, we intentionally focus our attention on the person speaking and make an effort not only to hear what he or she is saying, but to appreciate and understand what is being said. Listening requires effort and a genuine interest in the person who is speaking as well as his or her words.

When we listen intently to a person, we are saying, "You are a person of value whom I love and respect and what you have to say is important to me." Each of us receives great satisfaction from knowing we are speaking to someone who not only hears us but listens to us attentively.

Here is a good example of the difference between hearing and listening. It is the last play of the fourth quarter and your favorite team is lined up on the two yard line about to score the winning touchdown. At that precise instant, your wife calls out, "honey, would you please take out the garbage." You will hear her words but they won't register because you aren't listening—your attention is elsewhere. Your lack of response can easily be interpreted that you are intentionally ignoring your wife and refusing to listen to her. Not Good!!

Every person deserves to have us listen to him or her. This is especially true among fellow believers. As we are "quick to listen," our understanding of each other will deepen, our fellowship will become warmer, our appreciation for one another will increase, and our love for each other will grow.

Mar 10

Chuckle: *Why is it that when a door is open, it's ajar, but when a jar is open, it's not adoor?*

Quote: *"Anxiety does not empty tomorrow of its sorrows, But only empties today of its strength."* ~ Charles Haddon Spurgeon

Dealing with Anxiety

"Be anxious for nothing, but in everything by prayer and supplication, with thanksgiving, let your requests be known to God; and the peace of God, which surpasses all understanding, will guard your hearts and minds through Christ" (Philippians 4:6 NIV).

The New Living Translation renders the first phrase of our passage as, *"Don't worry about anything."* Worry has been defined as *"a small trickle of fear that meanders through the mind until it cuts a channel into which all other thoughts are drained."* Anxiety can literally incapacitate us and render us useless in life. Do worry, anxiety, stress, and restlessness rule your life? Do worry and anxiety keep you from being a happy and contented person?

In our society, worry contributes to stress which has been identified as a major cause of all sorts of physical and emotional disorders from coronary disease and strokes to obesity. But God's children are instructed, and given the resources, not to be anxious or worry. God is well aware of all the things in our lives that have the potential for causing anxiety, worry, and stress. In our passage today He uses the apostle Paul to teach us to react in a healthy way to these circumstances.

Paul was writing from prison. He was separated from

those he loved. Some were attempting to undermine and discredit all he had accomplished in starting churches. He was suffering physically and emotionally and was facing execution. Even in the face of these hardships, Paul said there would never be a crisis so severe and overwhelming that God would not bring peace even in the midst of it. Jesus said, *"Peace I leave with you; my peace I give you. I do not give to you as the world gives. Do not let your hearts be troubled and do not be afraid"* (John 14:27 NIV).

God has never promised to remove all the stresses of life, but He will always carry the load for you if only you will let Him do so. He wants each of us to experience the peace that surpasses all human understanding—a supernatural peace. This peace is for everyone that knows Christ as Savior and Lord. But if we aren't careful we will take the view that the troubles we are enduring are just too big and complicated to be accompanied by inner peace. To have this view is to limit God's power to work in your life. We're saying God can't do what He says He will do!

God's Word clearly indicates there is nothing you can face that is too big, difficult, troubling, or fearful for Him. In all circumstances, turn your worry, stress, and anxiety over to Him and His perfect peace will guard your heart. Paul tells us to turn our worries into prayers. Whenever you start to worry, stop and pray. Remember, *"Worry is like a rocking chair; it will give you something to do, but it won't get you anywhere!"*

Mar 11

Chuckle: *"A panhandler walked up to a well-dressed woman who was shopping on Main Street and said, 'Lady, I haven't eaten anything in four long days.'*

She looked at him and said, 'I wish I had your will power.'"

Quote: *"On my head pour only the sweet waters of serenity. Give me the gift of the Untroubled Mind."*
~ Joshua Loth Liebman

Grace and Peace

"Paul and Timothy, servants of Christ Jesus, To all the saints in Christ Jesus at Philippi . . . Grace and peace to you from God our Father and the Lord Jesus Christ" (Philippians 1:1-2 NIV).

Philippians is a letter from the apostle Paul to his dear Christian friends at Philippi. He called himself and his companion, Timothy, "servants of Jesus Christ." The term "servants" denotes dependence, obedience, intense devotion, and acknowledged ownership. In this letter, Paul reminded the Philippian Christians that the church is the living body of Christ and that they were partakers of His grace and peace. They were saints in the world but not of the world (see John 17:14-16). Their lives were hidden in Christ. Paul had a closer bond with the Philippian Christians than with any other church. He shared his circumstances as a Roman prisoner under house arrest, and the inner peace and joy which he enjoyed.

Paul sets forth a love relationship and a soul union between Christ and the believer. Perhaps the "in Christ" phrase was from Jesus when He talked about His being the vine and His followers being the branches in John 15. Union with Christ is accomplished by God's grace through faith—the channel through which God enters a person's inner being. Alfred Ackley's hymn conveys his personal testimony of the indwelling Christ in his life:

"He lives, He lives, Christ Jesus lives today! He walks with me and talks with me along life's narrow way. He lives, He lives, salvation to impart! You ask me how I know he lives: He lives within my heart."

Then Paul emphasizes the new life in Christ to refer to the believer's life fulfilled in the church (see 2 Cor. 5:17). Christ brought new life into the world by sharing His life with all people, and He brought new life to the world by starting a new community, the church.

All of us desire to experience genuine peace. Paul's salutation here is an exclamation, a declaration, a wish, and a prayer. "Grace and peace" are listed in their divine order and can never be reversed. There is no true peace without first experiencing God's grace. *"For it is by grace you have been saved, through faith"* (Ephesians 2:8 NIV). Peace follows the acceptance of God's grace through Jesus Christ. Someone has said, "Grace is the spring—peace is the stream flowing from the spring."

Mar 12

Bumper Snicker: *"I've taken a vow of poverty. To annoy me, send money."*

Quote: *"By compassion we make others' misery our own, and so, by relieving them, we relieve ourselves also."* ~ Sir Thomas Browne

Loving Crowds More Than People

"When Jesus came down from the mountainside, large crowds followed him. A man with leprosy came and knelt before him and said, 'Lord, if you are willing, you can make me clean.' Jesus reached out his hand and touched the man. 'I am willing,' he said. 'Be clean!' Immediately he was cured of his leprosy" (Matthew 8:1-3 NIV).

Earlier verses tell us that Jesus had been speaking to large crowds and they followed Him as He came down from the mountainside. It would have been easy for Jesus to ignore individual faces in the sea of humanity surrounding Him. But when a man with leprosy knelt before Him wanting to be healed, Jesus immediately showed love and compassion by giving the man His complete attention. The man was not lost in the crowd. This scene becomes even more remarkable when Jesus reaches out and touches the man who was declared unclean and shunned by society.

You can draw comfort from knowing that among the billions of people on this earth, Jesus is aware of you personally. He will never fail to see your face in the crowd. Even though Jesus died for a world of lost souls, He is your very personal Savior and Lord. From God's perspective, you will never be overlooked as just another face in the crowd. Oh what a valuable lesson each of us can learn from this passage.

All of us believers should love and pray for the untold millions of people around the world who need to hear the gospel message. But do we love that fellow worker, classmate, or neighbor down the street enough to pray specifically for that person and personally share Christ's love with him or her? Do we show our concern for the lost of the world by sitting in our easy chairs in front of our TVs and writing checks for missions, or do we care enough to get up, get out, get going, and do missions by ministering to the unique personal needs of individuals? Obviously, praying for and giving to missions are wonderful things, but if we see only the masses, we may become calloused and indifferent to the needs of individuals all around us.

Right now, you may need healing or cleansing in some area of your life. If so, please remember that Jesus knows you personally, and stands ready to meet those needs just like He did for the man with leprosy. You are not lost in the crowd. Out of love He will stretch out His hand and touch you. Shouldn't we follow His example? Like Jesus, we should always love each person in the crowd separately and individually and make time to minister to their physical, emotional, and spiritual needs. We must be careful that we don't love crowds more than people.

Chuckle: *"We need a responsible person,"* said the employer. *"I hope you fit that description?"*

"Yes, Sir, I'm your man," answered the potential employee. *"On my last job, every time anything went wrong, they said I was responsible."*

Quote: *"We cannot hold a torch to light another person's path without brightening our own."* ~ Ben Sweetland

Making Things New

"Therefore, if anyone is in Christ, he is a new creation; the old has gone, the new has come.... God made him who had no sin to be sin for us, so that in him we might become the righteousness of God" (2 Corinthians 5:17, 21 NIV).

I was born in Zinc, a small mining town in the mountains of North Arkansas. It was called "Zanc" by some of the locals. The town was located in a beautiful little valley with Sugar Orchard creek and the railroad running through it. As a child, I remember it being a bustling community with a several stores, a post office, a canning factory, and other businesses. My grandfather, and later my uncle, owned operated one of the grocery stores there. I thought it was the most wonderful place on earth.

However, today Zinc has grown old and there is almost nothing left of the community—just a few houses but no commerce of any kind. When I last visited the place, I couldn't help thinking how nice it would be if I could just snap my fingers and blow away the "oldness" and make it like it once was— make it new. But there's no way I can make the old town of Zinc new and there is no way I can make myself new. Only

God can do that and only He can make me acceptable in His sight.

In our passage, we see ourselves with our old sinful nature with no way for us to change our condition in our own strength. Our old nature has become polluted by sin and the standards of the world and is not a pretty sight in the eyes of God. In the same way it would take a "miracle" to make Zinc new again, it takes God's power to miraculously make us into new creations with new natures. It takes God's Holy Spirit remaking us once we repent of our sins and place our faith in the atoning sacrifice of Jesus Christ on the Cross. When we are "born again" as Jesus describes it, we are "in" Christ, and if we are in Christ, all things about us are made new. This means our lives and new nature are now controlled by the Spirit of God, not the lure of the world.

Does your life need a makeover to bring it into compliance with God's plan for you? Do you have the new nature that God wants to give you? If not, won't you bow your head this morning, give your heart and life to Jesus Christ, ask Him to forgive your sins, and make you into a new creation—a new person? Let Him make all things new and give you a new nature, a new purpose, a new joy, and a new peace.

Mar 14

Chuckle: *To begin a math class, the teacher asked, "What are 3, 6, 27, and 45?"*

Timmy quickly answered, "NBC, CBS, ESPN, and the Cartoon Network!"

Quote: *"Let there be kindness in your face, in your eyes, in your smile, in the warmth of your greeting . . . Don't only give your care, but give your heart as well."* ~ Mother Teresa

Keep It Simple

"Dear brothers and sisters, when I first came to you I didn't use lofty words and brilliant ideas to tell you God's message. For I decided to concentrate only on Jesus Christ and his death on the cross" (1 Corinthians 2:1-2 NLT).

Many Christians can be classified as brilliant Bible scholars. Their formal theological education, personal Bible study, and rich life experiences have given them deep insights into the difficult to understand Scriptures and the mind of Christ. The apostle Paul was such a man. He was a brilliant scholar and skilled orator who could have easily overwhelmed his listeners with impressive intellectual arguments. But he did not yield to the temptation to bring attention to himself by his impressive knowledge, understanding, and skill in articulating deep spiritual truths.

Instead, Paul kept it simple when conveying the gospel message to those he was trying to reach for Christ. He knew that the simple message of Jesus Christ and the cross expressed with the guidance and power of the Holy Spirit was the most effective way to communicate the gospel. He knew that the simple gospel *"is the power of God for the salvation of everyone who believes"* (Romans 1:16b NIV). Paul understood that we must make our message understandable to everyone if we are to be successful as Christ's ambassadors to a lost world.

Jesus made the gospel both profound and as simple as it gets, *"For God so loved the world (every human being) that he gave his one and only Son (Jesus), that whoever believes (has faith in, trusts) in him shall not perish but have eternal life"*(John 3:16 NIV).

We are wise if we follow Paul's example and keep the gospel message simple and basic for those we are trying to reach. Gregory the Great said, *"God first gathered the unlearned, afterwards philosophers, nor has He taught fisherman by orators, but has subdued orators by fishermen."* We should never depend upon our superior knowledge, understanding, or articulation skills to persuade people to come to Christ. We should use easily understood terms and depend upon the Holy Spirit to add power to our words.

Obviously, Paul does not diminish the importance of formal education and study of the Scriptures for Christians. However, his confidence was not in his superior intellect or speaking abilities, but in the power of the Spirit. Paul's statement about making the message simple and basic should never be used as an excuse for not studying and preparing before preaching or teaching.

Mar 15

Chuckle: T*eacher: "Phil, who was the first woman?"*
Phil: "I don't know."
Teacher: "Here's a hint. It had something to do with an apple."
Phil: "Oh, I know. Granny Smith."
Quote: *"No clever arrangement of bad eggs ever made a good omelet."* ~ C. S. Lewis

A Good Omelet

"Just as our bodies have many parts and each part has a special function, so it is with Christ's body. We are parts of his one body, and each of us has different work to do. And since we are all one body in Christ, we belong to each other, and each of us needs all the others" (Romans 12:4-5 NIV). *"The body is a unit, though it is made up of many parts; and though all its parts are many, they form one body"* (1 Corinthians 12:12 NIV).

I must admit I had never thought to use eggs and omelet as an illustration for describing a healthy church—that is until I ran across the above C. S. Lewis quote. It reminded me of a central Biblical truth—the body of Christ, the church, is comprised of many individual Christians, each of which is essential to the health of the church. *"From him (Jesus) the whole body, joined and held together by every supporting ligament, grows and builds itself up in love as each part (member) does its work"* (Ephesians 4:16 NIV). However, if some of the members are "bad eggs," the church will never be what Christ intended it to be—a "good omelet," pleasing to our Lord. To put it another way: the quality of the church is dependent upon the spiritual condition and contribution of its individual members.

There are many things we can do in an effort to compensate for the spiritual inadequacies of church members. However, no matter how many times we reorganize or rearrange the members, it is, ultimately, the condition of the hearts of individual members that will determine the condition of the church as a whole. Rearranging a church of bad eggs is like rearranging the deck chairs on the Titanic—both are exercises in futility. Let's consider this question: does my faithfulness to our Lord and His church qualify me as a good egg contributing toward making my church what God wants her to be—a good omelet?

What "bad egg" attitudes can seriously damage the fellowship and effectiveness of the church? Here are a few for your consideration: My personal contribution to the ministry of the church is not important. I don't have the ability to do anything significant to strengthen my church. I don't need to attend church to have a good relationship with God. I don't like the way the church is being run, so, I choose not to participate. Someone hurt my feelings so I'm dropping out of the church.

You get the idea. If we don't want to do something, one excuse is as good another.

But what a beautiful thing it is to see a church where, in the power of the Holy Spirit, all its members are actively contributing to its loving fellowship and effective ministries—a congregation of "good eggs" working together to produce a "good omelet" for the glory of our Lord.

Chuckle: *"Two times a week, my wife and I go to a nice restaurant, have a little beverage, good food and companionship. She goes on Tuesdays, I go on Fridays."* ~ Red Skelton

Quote: *"Is prayer your steering wheel or your spare tire?"* ~ *Corrie Ten Boom*

Praying in Secret

"And when you pray, do not be like the hypocrites, for they love to pray standing in the synagogues and on the street corners to be seen of men. . . . But when you pray, go into your room, close the door and pray to your Father. . . Then your Father, who sees what is done in secret, will reward you" (Matthew 6:5-6 NIV).

In His Sermon on the Mount, Jesus makes a basic assumption in giving these instructions to His disciples and to us: that His disciples, and we, would pray. Notice He said "when" you pray, not "if" you pray. Jesus was telling us that prayer should be a natural part of being a Christian.

Jesus gives us some basic instructions on how we should pray to make our prayers acceptable to the Father. He warns us of the danger of being a hypocrite when it comes to prayer. Hypocrites appear to be something they aren't. They are play acting. They are wearing a mask. Perhaps they appear to be something on Sunday that differs from what they are during the week. Jesus says they are more interested in men hearing their prayers than God, thus drawing attention to themselves instead of the Father.

Jesus' teaching here reminds me of an iceberg analogy. Approximately ten percent of an iceberg is visible above the water. Ninety percent cannot be seen because it's under the water. This is how our spiritual lives should be. We should spend ninety percent of our prayer time out of the sight of others, never drawing attention to ourselves. The ten percent of our spiritual lives that people see should be the result of the ninety percent that only God sees as we fellowship with Him.

We can glean some basic truths from being genuine in our prayers and Christian living: It gives credibility to our witness—we are believable because we're real and genuine. Praying in secret results in the rewards of having God hear and answer our prayers. This is because we will pray in the will of God—not for our will to be done.

This kind of secret Bible study and prayer will help us experience the joy of God's presence in our lives because our relationship and fellowship with Him is our primary goal —not to impress those around us with our piety. This passage does not prohibit public prayers, but deals with the attitude of the heart when we pray. Upon whose ears do we want our prayers to fall?

"Little of the Word with little prayer is death to the spiritual life. Much of the Word with little prayer gives a sickly life. Much prayer with little of the Word gives emotional life. But a full measure of both the Word and prayer each day gives a healthy and powerful life." ~ Andrew Murray

Mar 17

Chuckle: *"Never trust a faith healer who limps!"*
Quote: *"A Christian should be a walking sermon, a breathing prayer, a living poem, a visible spirit, and a human candle."*
~ William Arthur Ward

Reflecting the Light

When Jesus spoke again to the people, he said, "I am the light of the world. Whoever follows me will never walk in darkness, but will have the light of life" (John 8:12 NIV).

Many years ago I received a guided tour through Diamond Cave in North Arkansas. With the cavern completely lighted, many beautiful and varied rock formations were visible. But the guide wanted us to experience the total darkness within the cave, and at the deepest point underground he turned off the lights. Up to that point, I thought I knew what darkness was, but I was wrong. I had never experienced such inky blackness before. It was horrible! I came away with a new appreciation for light that dispels the darkness.

We know that the sun is the source of physical light on earth. The moon only reflects the sun's light, and has no inherent light of its own. When I move my thoughts out of the physical realm and into the spiritual realm, an amazing corollary takes shape. In our passage, Jesus declares that He is the Light of the World, but in Matthew 5:14, He says to us, *"You are the light of the world."* And in John 1:6-9, the Apostle John referred to John the Baptist this way, *"There came a man who was sent from God; his name was John. He came as a witness to testify concerning that Light (Jesus), so that through him men might believe. He himself was not the light; he came only as a witness to the light. The true light that gives light to every man (person) was coming into the world."*

Along with John the Baptist, we followers of Christ are not the light of the world, but are to allow His light to shine through us. As the moon only reflects the light of the sun, our lives are to reflect the light of the Son. In the same way the lights dispelled physical darkness in that cave, so Christ dispels the spiritual darkness in the hearts of people. And when Jesus calls us the light of the world, He knows we have no light of our own but are only reflectors of His light to others.

In the same way that the reflected light by the moon casts light upon the earth at night, our lives can reflect the light of Christ into the lives of those around us. Without the light of Jesus, there is total spiritual darkness in the hearts of people. The problem is that sometimes pride makes us want to be the light rather than a reflector of the Light—the lamp through whom the light shines. Speaking of His light shining through us, Jesus said, *"Let your light so shine before men that they may see your good deeds and praise your Father in heaven"* (Matthew 5:16).

Mar 18

Chuckle: *A preacher said to a very dignified lady at a wedding— "Are you a friend of the groom?"*
She replied, "I should say not. I'm the mother of the bride."
Quote: *"Of all the causes which conspire to blind Man's erring judgment, and misguide the mind; What the weak head with strongest bias rules,— Is pride, the never-failing vice of fools."* ~ Alexander Pope

Perils of Pride

"So do we have a reason to brag about ourselves? No! And why not? It is the way of faith that stops all bragging, not the way of trying to obey the law" (Romans 3:27 NIV).

Many Christians are like the woodpecker who was pecking away on the trunk of a dead tree. Suddenly lightning struck the tree and splintered it. The woodpecker flew away unharmed. Looking back to where the dead tree had stood, the proud bird exclaimed, "Look what I did!"

Pride is undue confidence in and attention to one's own skills, position, accomplishments, or possessions. Pride is easier to recognize than to define, and easier to recognize in others than in oneself. Many biblical words describe this concept, each with its own emphasis. Some other words for pride include arrogance, presumption, conceit, self-satisfaction, boasting, and high-mindedness.

Pride in humans has been around since Adam and Eve. It inspired their disobedience of God. It is always with us and is the basis of all sin. A common form pride is the pride of privilege. When a person is given a special position, he/she forgets that it was given and becomes proud, as if his own works had earned the victory. God knows man's heart and made many references to the perils which accompany pride. *"Pride and arrogance and the evil way and the perverted mouth, I hate"* (Proverbs 8:13 NIV).

I think God has so much to say about pride because, ultimately, a prideful person is saying, "I don't need God—I can handle my life on my own." As our Creator and Sustainer, God has the perfect plan laid out before us. Our attempting to "go it alone" will only lead us down a path of disappointment and self-destruction. No one knows that better than God. He has seen pride destroy the lives of His creations throughout history. *Pride goes before destruction, a haughty spirit before a fall"* (Proverbs 16:18 NIV).

If pride is an issue in your life, ask God to remove the focus from yourself and return to a healthy focus on Him. Leave your trappings of pride, ego, and accomplishments behind so you may stand in His presence without fear of being rebuked. Pride won't find a foothold in a heart that sees its sinful state and its need for God's grace and mercy.

When the nineteenth-century American evangelist, Asahel Nettleton, was asked what he considered the best safeguard against spiritual pride, he replied: "I know of nothing better than to keep my eye on my great sinfulness."

Mar 19

Chuckle - Child's prayer: *"Dear God, if Cain and Abel had their own rooms, maybe they wouldn't kill each other. It works with me and my brother." Larry*

Quote: *"Self-respect and a clear conscience are powerful components of integrity and are the basis for enriching your relationships with others."* ~ Denis Waitley

Healthy Relationships

"So in everything, do to others what you would have them do to you . . . ." (Matthew 7:12 NIV). *"Be devoted to one another in brotherly love. Honor one another above yourselves"* (Romans 12:10 NIV).

Healthy relationships are essential for a happy and fulfilled life. However, many have accumulated wealth by walking over and mistreating family, friends, and employees; and then, in old age, they come to realize they are devoid of meaningful relationships. Without the stimulation of healthy relationships, we can easily become lonely, bitter, and angry. God intends for us to first have a joyful love relationship with Him and then with others. He knows warm and rewarding relationships are vital to our joy, peace, and contentment. So He gave us this principle to use in everyday life.

It sounds so simple and is often called "The Golden Rule," but it's not a rule at all. It's a principle, or truth, to be lived out. It's something you weave into the very fabric of your life. It has been memorized by many, but lived out by few. Today, let God's Spirit shake us awake and make us live out this truth. I see this "golden" principle as the summation of all the Bible has to say on the subject of interpersonal relationships.

If we were committed to this principle, by the power of the Holy Spirit, it would revolutionize our circle of relationships. If fifty of your neighbors would do this it would change your community. If all of us did, it would change our whole county— a powerful reality—a dynamic truth. This principle requires each of us to take the initiative in relationship building and not wait to see how others treat us. God wants it to become a part of our regenerated nature and an action rather than a reaction. John Maxwell said this, *"Instead of putting others in their place, put yourself in their place."* Jesus practiced this principle: Everyone He met was a VIP. He treated them as special no matter their status in life. He cared about them and wants us to do likewise.

Do you treat your spouse, children, and other family members the way you want them to treat you? Do you show them they are important by the way you relate to them? Many of us even treat casual acquaintances better than our own family members. This is a Christian crime.

What about our enemies? The Golden Rule principle is to be applied to everyone, not just a select few. "But," you say, "they didn't treat me that way?" That's the point of this verse— believers are to be different. This principle says we treat others the way we want to be treated, not the way they treat us. When our treatment of others is consistent with the Golden Rule principle, precious, lasting relationships and friendships will result.

Mar 20

Chuckle: A child's prayer: *"Dear God, Did you intend for the giraffe to look like that or was it an accident?"* Norma

Quote: *"Trust is to human relationships what faith is to gospel living. It is the beginning place, the foundation upon which more can be built. Where trust is, love can flourish."*
~ Barbara B. Smith

A Difficult Principle in Relationships

"Here is a simple, rule-of-thumb guide for behavior: Ask yourself what you want people to do for you, then grab the initiative and do it for them. Add up God's Law and Prophets and this is what you get" (Matthew 7:12 MSG).

Living by the Golden Rule principle is impossible in our own strength. How then can we say to a skeptical world, "if we would only treat each other like we want to be treated," the world would be a better place?" This is a principle to live by for believers who have been changed from the inside out. When Jesus spoke these words, He was teaching His followers in His Sermon on the Mount. To fully understand and apply His words to in our daily living requires a transformation by the Holy Spirit. *"Therefore, if anyone is in Christ, he is a new creation; the old has gone, the new has come!"* (2 Corinthians 5:17 NIV).

A missionary was sharing Matthew 7:12 with some natives. When he finished, the head of the group said, "If the God who made us would give us a new heart, then we could do this, but that's the only way." Only if we have a new heart can this principle be applied as Jesus intends. William Barkley said, *"To obey this principle, a man must become a new man with a new center to his life."* Families and churches have been torn apart because people wouldn't treat one another as they want to be treated.

To be true to the teachings of Jesus, we must never apply the Golden Rule principle solely to get better treatment for ourselves. It should always be applied out of Christ-like love and compassion for others and to make their lives better. More than likely, it will result in better treatment for ourselves, but that should not be our motive. Agape—Christ-like—love for others is unconditional. It expects nothing in return.

Here is a challenge for each of us today: First, be sure you have trusted Jesus Christ as Savior and Lord. Then pray every day for the power to treat the people in your life with love, kindness, consideration, understanding, and acceptance in the same way you want to be treated. Ask God to help you refocus on building relationships.

If you do this, your life and the lives of those around you will change dramatically and you will be happier and more completely fulfilled. One of the most difficult things to give away is kindness, for it is usually returned in even greater measure than that which was given.

Mar 21

Chuckle: *"Pride is the only disease known to man that makes everyone else sick except the one who has it."*

Quote: *"Look out how you use proud words. When you let proud words go, it is not easy to call them back. They wear long boots, hard boots . . . Look out how you use proud words."*
~ Carl Sandburg

Proud Words

"Pride goes before destruction, a haughty spirit before a fall. Better to be lowly in spirit and among the oppressed than to share plunder with the proud" (Proverbs 16:18-19 NIV).

Ingrid Bergman, the stage and screen star, said this about proud words, *"There is in the words of Carl Sandburg a primary lesson for individuals and classes and nations alike. All too often, we say the cruel and destructive things—because it is so much easier to be clever than to be kind. But in the long run, proud and angry words are the ones which cause trouble in our homes, our communities and among nations. Proud words are arrogant, intolerant and savagely ignorant of the great fundamental truths—simplicity, humility and ordinary human decency. They are indeed rough-shod, and it is not easy to call them back."*

Our proverbs passage makes it clear that pride can be ruinous in our lives and leads to a disastrous outcome. When we add the words of James to the equation, the danger of a prideful spirit and arrogant and uncontrolled words becomes abundantly clear. *"If anyone considers himself religious and yet does not keep a tight rein on his tongue, he deceives himself and his religion is worthless"* (James 1:26 NIV).

Pride is a deceitful thing. It deceives the proud person into thinking he is not prideful. We can go through life never recognizing that we have it, and wonder why people react to us the way they do. As a Christian, a regular pride check-up, based on God's Word, is essential if our words are to be encouraging, uplifting and edifying to those around us. Proud people pay little attention to their weaknesses and are often not aware of stumbling blocks that beset others because the proud person thinks he or she is above the frailties of other people.

Although those around them may be keenly aware of their pride problem, the prideful person may not even be aware of it. The proud suffer from a distorted self-image. They exaggerate their own importance and see others in a lessor light. Such pride feeds condescension, rudeness, and even prejudice. Our proud words are only a symptom of what's going on in our prideful heart, and the solution is a heart makeover which will be reflected in our words and actions.

Jesus said, *"The good man (person) brings good things out of the good stored in his heart, and the evil man brings evil things out of the evil stored up in his heart. For out of the overflow of his heart his mouth speaks"* (Luke 6:45 NIV).

Mar 22

Chuckle: *A visiting official made a phone call from a mental institution and had difficulty getting his number. Finally, he shouted at the operator, "Do you know who I am?"*
    "No," she replied calmly, "but I know where you are."
    Quote: *"Our safety lies in God and not in our feeling safe."*
~ Hubert van Zeller

Anchor for Our Souls

"This confidence (in God's promises) is like a strong and trustworthy anchor for our souls. It leads us through the curtain of heaven into God's inner sanctuary" (Hebrews 6:19 NLT).

The word "anchor" only appears four times in the entire Bible. Three times it is used in Luke's account of fierce storms at sea (see Acts 27:29-30, 40). The other is in our passage. It's interesting that the anchor cross was one of the signs used by early Christians to signify their hope and faith.

There are many situations in the Christian life when using the analogy of a ship's anchor is highly appropriate. It provides us encouragement and strengthens our confidence that God is our never-failing anchor. A ship's anchor is designed to hold the ship fast and secure even through pounding waves, strong undercurrents, and ferocious winds.

As we go through each day, and sometimes endure difficult storms, we must decide in whom—or in what—we trust to provide us anchorage and stability. It is Jesus Christ who provides an anchor for our souls and He is our connection (anchor) to the Father.

Because God embodies all truth, He cannot lie. Therefore, we can be secure in every promise He makes in His Word. His promises provide the stability for your life in the same way that a ship's anchor holds firmly to the seabed. Jesus says He is the way to the Father. *"I am the way, and the truth, and the life. No one comes to the Father except through me"* (John 14:6 NIV). It is through faith in Him that we are saved. Also, it is through Him that we have access to the Father in our prayers. It is through Him that we have a reliable anchor even when everything around us is coming apart.

Neal A. Maxwell put it this way: Our *"Ultimate hope constitutes the anchor of the soul."* The lyrics of an old hymn go like this: *"Be very sure, Be very sure your anchor holds and grips the solid rock."*

Mar 23

Chuckle: *"Why are retirees so slow to clean out the basement, attic, or garage? They know that as soon as they do, one of their adult kids will store stuff there. "*

Quote: *"If you don't change your beliefs, your life will be like this forever. Is that good news?"* ~ Dr. Robert Anthony

What You Believe Matters

"There is a way that seems right to a man, but in the end it leads to death ... A simple man believes anything, but a prudent man gives thought to his steps" (Proverbs 14:12, 15 NIV).

Some say, "It really doesn't matter what you believe as long as you are sincere." Or, "we are all trying to get to heaven in our own way." The implication is that there are many different beliefs and actions that will qualify you for heaven when you die. For many years, some of the best minds in the world sincerely believed the world was flat. They were sincerely wrong. It does matter what you believe and there is only one source of truth for living, God Himself through His Word. Jesus said, *"I am the way and the truth and the life. No one comes to the Father except through me"* (John 14: 6 NIV).

What you believe will determine how you live. *"Above all else, guard your heart, for it affects everything you do"* (Proverbs 4:23 NLT). We all live by our beliefs and our value systems. What we believe to be true becomes our guide for our actions and relationships. If you sincerely believe you can earn your way to heaven just by living a good moral life, you will spend your life trying to be good and living with the uncertainty of whether or not you measure up. You will be sincerely wrong. However, if you have placed your faith in the

Truth Himself, Jesus Christ, you will have assurance of eternal life and your life will be marked by obedience to Him and adherence to His teachings.

What you believe is your choice. *"They exchanged the truth of God for a lie, and worshiped and served created things rather than the Creator"* (Romans 1:25 NIV). Each of us must choose what we believe. If we accept opinions, half-truths, and outright lies as truth, we may sincerely believe them sincerely wrong. To not make a choice is a choice to reject Jesus Christ. We cannot be neutral in decisions that determine our eternal destiny. Before you accept something to be true and make it a part of your belief system, first compare it to what God's Word has to say about it. *"I, the LORD, speak the truth; I declare what is right"* (Isaiah 45:19b NIV). It does matter what we believe.

"Salvation is found in no one else, for there is no other name under heaven given to men by which we must be saved" (Acts 4:12 NIV). *"Whoever believes in the Son has eternal life, but whoever rejects the son will not see life, for God's wrath remains on him"* (John 3:36 NIV). *"While driving, you encounter a sign that reads, 'Dangerous Curve Ahead.' Immediately you are confronted with a choice. One, you can observe the warning and slow down. Two, you can ignore the warning and maintain your speed. Or, three, you can defy the warning and speed up. Whatever your response, you will not change the truth of the sign. The curve remains dangerous, regardless of whether you acknowledge the fact or not."* ~ Illustrations for Biblical Preaching; by Michael P. Green

Mar 24

Chuckle: *"A thoughtful wife has steaks ready when her husband comes home from a fishing trip!"*

Quote: *"He who is filled with love is filled with God himself."* ~ St. Augustine of Hippo

Bridges of Love

"Do to others as you would have them do to you. If you love those who love you, what credit is that to you? Even sinners love those who love them. And if you do good to those who are good to you, what credit is that to you? Even sinners do that" (Luke 6:31-33 NIV).

In 1851, James Robling made the shocking announcement that he would build a bridge across the Niagara River Gorge. Engineers said it was impossible. The span was 800 feet. The height was 200 feet. Water flowed over the falls at 37 million gallons per minute and rushed down the gorge. It would be impossible to set piers to support the bridge. But he built a suspension bridge so strong that trains could pass over it.

Jesus is the greatest bridge-builder of all time—across time and space—from heaven to earth—from sin to salvation. Jesus is saying to Christians, "I want you to be like me. I want you to build bridges to others so they can walk across that bridge of your life to me." As bridge builders, we must learn two major lessons:

First, we must learn to think like Jesus. Philippians 2:5 says, *"Let this mind be in you that is also in Christ Jesus."* We must allow His Spirit to give us the mind of Christ. Like Jesus, we must invest ourselves in the lives of others. Jesus said, *"As the Father has sent me, so I'm sending you."* Jesus said, you're "salt and the light." Both of these must be put to use to have value. Salt can't season unless it is poured out. Light is useless if kept in a closet. God wants us to:

~ Have Christ's love for hurting people. *"When he (Jesus) saw the crowds, he had compassion on them, because they were harassed and helpless, like sheep without a shepherd"* (Matthew 9:36 NIV). The lost and hurting are the ones to which Jesus is referring; sick, hurting, hungry, naked, alone, etc.

~ Adopt Jesus' methods. Luke 6:36 says, *"Be merciful, just as your Father is merciful."* Galatians 6:10 says, *"Let us do good to all people."* Bridges have one purpose—they connect and allow people to move from one place to another. When we build bridges of love, we say, "don't come to our church; we're coming to you." A small act of kindness says I love you, and there's a God who loves you.

Second, we must act like Jesus. Our motives must be pure and our love proven. James said in 2:17 NIV, *"In the same way, faith by itself, not accompanied by action is dead. . . I will show you my faith by what I do."* Jesus came from heaven to build a bridge of love between us and the Father—Jesus is that bridge, and we should be bridges to others. Acts of kindness in Jesus' name can have amazing impact on those who have not experienced God's love. If you want to make a difference in your children, take them to where they can help someone who is hungry, sick, old, alone. If we learn to think and act like Jesus, we will build bridges of love to those around us.

Mar 25

Chuckle: *"Birthdays are good for you—the more you have, the longer you live!"*

Quote: *"I am a citizen, not of Athens or Greece, but of the world."* ~ Socrates

Christian Citizenship

The Great Commission from Jesus: *"Therefore go and make disciples of all nations, baptizing them in the name of the Father and of the Son and of the Holy Spirit, and teaching them to obey everything I have commanded you. And surely I am with you always to the very end of the age"* (Matthew 28:19-20 NIV).

Socrates, an ancient Greek philosopher, is thought by many to be one of the wisest men who ever lived. Of course, God gave Solomon *"a wise and discerning heart so that there will never have been anyone like you, nor will there ever be"* (1 Kings 3:12 NIV). As a wise man, Socrates accepted personal responsibility as a global citizen. Citizenship is a term that implies obedience to the laws and authorities that govern us; social interaction and cooperation with other people; responsibility for the wellbeing of our fellow human beings; and a desire to make our society and the world a better place for all people.

According to Scripture, Christians have dual citizenship. We are citizens of this earthly world, but more important, we are citizens of God's kingdom of heaven. As citizens of this world, we are responsible to those who govern us (see Romans 13) and also to our fellow citizens. As citizens in God's kingdom, we are governed by God's Word, which includes the Great Commission. *". . . our citizenship is in heaven. And we eagerly await a Savior from there, the Lord Jesus Christ. . ."*

(Philippians 3:20 NIV). *". . . you are no longer foreigners or aliens, but fellow citizens with God's people and members of God's household"* (Ephesians 2:19 NIV).

As Christian citizens, we sometimes have a very narrow view of our responsibilities as citizens, limiting our concern to our immediate family and local community. The great commission, from the lips of Jesus Himself, fixes our responsibility as global, spiritual citizens. If we are obedient, we cannot share Christ with only a specific segment of the population. Jesus further illuminated our global citizenship responsibility in Acts 1:8, *"you will be my witnesses in Jerusalem, and in all Judea and Samaria, and to the ends of the earth."*

In my home church, a certain week each year is designated as a Week of Prayer for International (global) Missions. We emphasize our responsibilities to pray for missionaries around the world and to give to our annual international missions offering. Your church may have a similar emphasis; but if not, you can certainly pray and give on an individual basis. We must be responsible citizens, in both the spiritual and physical realms, and your faithfulness is critical if God's plan for our world and His kingdom is to become reality.

Mar 26

Chuckle: Kid's Lyrics: *"God bless America, through the night with a light from a bulb!"*

Quote: *"Choose Jesus Christ! Deny yourself, take up the 'Cross, and follow Him for the world must be shown. The world must see, in us, a discernible, visible, startling difference."*
~ Elisabeth Elliott

A Cleansed Life

"You used to walk in these ways, in the life you once lived. But now you must rid yourselves of all such things as these: anger, rage, malice, slander, and filthy language from your lips. . . Clothe yourselves with compassion, kindness, humility, gentleness and patience" (Colossians 3:7-8, 12 NIV).

I'm often amazed by the open display of anger and rage in our society. Sadly, Christians are not immune to these types of sins, and we can see by our Scripture passage that such actions are not unique to our time. Out of control anger can cause people to do horrible things to one another. Anger and jealousy caused Cain to kill his brother Abel (see Genesis 4). Uncontrolled anger causes parents to abuse their children. Anger causes husbands and wives to mistreat one another and destroys marriages. Anger results in the sinful actions listed in our passage—and all sorts of abhorrent behaviors.

When we are born again in Christ, we are cleansed of our sins and become God's new creations (see 2 Cor. 5:17). The Holy Spirit takes up residence in our lives and gives us the strength we need to avoid the terrible results of anger, rage, etc. However, when we allow selfishness, greed, and self-centeredness to creep into our lives, we are headed for disaster. Here Paul is urging believers to remain true to our faith, and rid ourselves of our old lives clothing ourselves in our God-given new nature in Christ.

Do you sometimes catch yourself telling a lie or half-truth to get what you want or to hurt someone toward whom you have hard feelings? Have you gossiped or slandered someone's character out of anger? Every Christian is a life-long work in progress and the more we come to know Christ, the more we are being changed to be like Him. Simply stated, clothing yourself with a brand new nature means that your conduct should match your faith. We should act like people of God. This is a straightforward step that is as simple as putting on your clothes each day. Clothe yourself in the righteousness of Christ and live in the power of the Holy Spirit.

If you drift into the sins mentioned in our passage, please remember that God is a God of forgiveness and cleansing, *"If we confess our sins, He is faithful and just and will forgive us our sins and purify (cleanse) us from all unrighteousness"* (1 John 1:9 NIV).

Karl Menninger, a famous psychiatrist, says that if he could convince the patients in his psychiatric hospitals that their sins are forgiven, seventy-five percent of them could walk out the next day. We often fail to take God at His word that our lives can be cleansed and our sins forgiven—wiped away forever.

Let God cleanse your life and then clothe yourself with Christ-likeness, including compassion, kindness, humility, gentleness and patience.

Mar 27

Chuckle: A cop to a speeder: *"Yeah, we have a quota... Two more tickets and my wife gets a toaster oven!"*

Ponder This: *"Changing the way people act is the fruit of repentance."* ~ Rick Warren

Cleansing and Usefulness

"Then one of the seraphs flew to me with a live coal in his hand, which he had taken with tongs from the altar. With it he touched my mouth and said, 'See, this has touched your lips; your guilt is taken away and your sin atoned for'" (Isaiah 6:6-7 NIV).

When Isaiah found himself in God's presence, he saw himself as wretchedly sinful and unworthy to behold the holiness of God. He cried out in despair, *"Woe to me for I am ruined! I am a man of unclean lips."* His repentant cry of desperation and confession led God to forgive him and cleanse him.

When Isaiah saw himself as sinful before God, with no hope of measuring up to God's standard of holiness, he became a worthy candidate for action on God's part. He saw himself as unclean and spiritually bankrupt. But when he reached this level of repentance and confession, he became a recipient of God's miraculous forgiveness and cleansing. When the live coal touched his lips, he was told that his sins were forgiven by the power of a merciful God.

In response to God's forgiveness and cleansing, Isaiah submitted himself completely to God's will and his service. No matter how difficult the task, he was willing to go and do whatever God asked of him. The cleansing process was necessary before he could fulfil the task to which God was calling him—before he could be useful to God. Before you or I accept God's call to speak and act for Him, we must be cleansed as Isaiah was by confessing our sins and submitting to God's control. Submitting ourselves and allowing God to purify us can be painful, but we must be purified before we are worthy to truly represent a pure and holy God.

I am reminded of a quote from a friend of D. L. Moody that went something like this, *"The world has yet to see what God can do through a man totally committed to Him. With God's help and grace, I will be that man."* These words may not be an exact quote, but the essence is there. This was Isaiah's attitude after God had forgiven and purified him. As he began to more clearly see God, the more aware he became of his own inadequacy and powerlessness to do anything of lasting value without God.

If you are a Christian, God has forgiven your sins and cleansed you with a definite purpose in mind for your life. But the sins of disobedience and indifference may have crept into your life. If so, please hear these words, *"If we confess our sins, he is faithful and just and will forgive us our sins and purify (cleanse) us from all unrighteousness"* (1 John 1:9 NIV).

Are you ready and available to be used by God regardless of where He chooses to send you or what He asks you to do?

Mar 28

Chuckle: *A child's prayer: "Dear God, is it true my father won't get in Heaven if he uses his golf words in the house?"* Anita

Quote: *"There is a comfort in the strength of love: 'Twill make a thing endurable, which else would overset the brain, or break the heart."* ~ William Wordsworth

Comforting Others

"All praise to the God and Father of our Lord Jesus Christ. He is the source of every mercy and the God who comforts us. He comforts us in all our troubles so that we can comfort others. When others are troubled, we will be able to give them the same comfort God has given us" (2 Corinthians 1:3-4 NLT).

No doubt there have been times in your life when you desperately needed a hug and a comforting word to help you through a difficult time or situation. We all have. If you are a Christian, you are fully aware of the comfort that comes from our Lord, even in the worst of times. We must keep in mind, however, that God's comfort does not always mean the troubles will go away, but that He gives us the strength and courage to endure the pain.

God comforts us because He loves us and genuinely cares about what happens to us. However, please notice in our passage that God has a deeper purpose in His comforting us— to prepare us to comfort someone else who is suffering through a time of trouble and heartache. It's good to keep in mind that every trial God allows you to experience will help prepare you to comfort others who are suffering in similar ways. It gives you the ability to identify, sympathize, and empathize with them. When someone offers comfort to you, it means much more if you know that person has experienced a similar trial. It gives credibility to their efforts to comfort you. You know they understand.

God's comfort provides us a model to use when we reach out to others. He teaches us to reach out in His grace and compassion. Often we cannot remove the pain from our friend's life, but we suffer through the experience with them and offer them the same comfort God has so lovingly and graciously given us. Sometimes a person just needs someone to share their troubles with—someone to listen.

A little girl lost a playmate to death and one day reported to her family that she had gone to comfort the sorrowing mother. "What did you say?" asked her parents. "Nothing," she replied. "I just climbed up on her lap and cried with her."

When others show tender compassion to the point of shedding tears on your behalf, their comfort can bring you inexplicable peace and contentment even in the worst of times. Let's look for opportunities to comfort those around us who are hurting. When you look outside yourself and comfort others, you will be amazed at how much comfort you receive in return.

Mar 29

Chuckle: *"Most people gain weight by having intimate dinners for two—alone."*

Quote: *"Sweet are the thoughts that savour of content; The quiet mind is richer than a crown."* ~ Robert Greene

Being Content in All Circumstances

". . . . for I have learned to be content whatever the circumstances. . . . I have learned the secret of being content in any and every situation, whether well fed or hungry, whether living in plenty or in want. I can do everything through him who gives me strength" (Philippians 4:11-12 NIV).

Two little teardrops were floating down the river of life. One asked the other, "Who are you?" "I'm a teardrop from a girl who loved a man and lost him. But who are you?" The first teardrop replied, "I'm a teardrop from the girl who got him!" Life is like that. We cry for things we can't have, but we might cry twice as hard if we had received them. Jesus spoke often of qualities that produce contentment and peace. Are you content with your life? Do others think of you when they name contented people?

I am convinced that it is a greater challenge to be content while having much and trying to use it properly with a Christ-like spirit, than it is while having little. Often it seems that the more we have, the more we want—never quite satisfied or content. Notice that Paul said, *"I have learned the secret of being content."* Contentment is not a trait that comes to us naturally. It is a supernatural condition available to the Christian who has learned its secret.

Learning to be content is a process which takes time. You

can't expect to master skiing or golf the first time you try. You must learn. Paul said he had learned to be content even while in prison chains. His contentment did not depend on external circumstances. In 2 Corinthians 11:24-27, he noted the terrible circumstances in which he learned how to be content. His tutor was the "God of peace."

Contentment doesn't mean you necessarily like your circumstances. It means you have confidence that God is involved with you in them. It's the surrender of yourself into His care. We have to accept the fact that God is in control not us. We must move from "my timing, my way, my outcome" to "God's timing, God's way, God's outcome." It's all about Christ. With Christ we can learn to say, *"I can do everything (including being content) through Christ who gives me strength."* It is Christ's power that lets us to rise above our worrisome, frustrating circumstances and say, "It is well with my soul."

"A story is told of a king who was suffering from a mysterious ailment and was advised by his astrologer that he would be cured if the shirt of a contented man was brought for him to wear. People went out to all parts of the kingdom looking for such a person, and after a long search they found a man who was really happy. But he did not have a shirt."

Mar 30

Chuckle: *"In 1920 the U. S. Post Office ruled that children could not be sent by parcel post. Makes you wonder what was going on before the ruling!"*

Quote: *"Courage faces fear and thereby masters it. Cowardice represses fear and is thereby mastered by it."* ~ Martin Luther King

Courage under Fire

"The members of the council were amazed when they saw the boldness of Peter and John, for they could see that they were ordinary men with no special training in the Scriptures. They also recognized them as men who had been with Jesus" (Acts 4:13 NLT).

To say that a soldier "showed courage under enemy fire" is a great compliment. But there are many types of enemy fire, much of which come from Satan himself. There are those who would silence us from proclaiming the gospel message of Jesus Christ and would like to see our society totally free from religious influences. It seems there is growing animosity toward Christians and our freedom to express our values and to worship freely may become threatened. We must be bold and courageous even in the face of threatening opposition, and we can take courage from the lives of early New Testament Christians like Peter and John.

In our text, the ruling religious leaders of Israel were doing everything in their power to silence the powerful voices of those proclaiming the message of Jesus Christ. Many were beaten, imprisoned, and even killed for their actions. When you face ridicule and persecution for expressing your faith, take heart because you are not alone. And you are not dependent upon your own strength to see you through.

The boldness and courage of Peter and John caused great consternation in the minds of the ruling Jewish council. They were amazed that these unschooled and ordinary men were so powerful and articulate in preaching their message. When you feel you are just too "ordinary" to be used of God, forget it. That's the Devil speaking to you. In our day and time, Our Lord needs every Christian to act and speak boldly, in love, as we defend our faith and as we work to elect leaders who will protect our freedoms to do so.

Your power to act and speak boldly is the same power evidenced in the courage of Peter and John. When our lives reflect the characteristics of Jesus in the power of the Spirit, those around us will be amazed by what God is doing through us. A changed life convinces people of Christ's power. One of your greatest testimonies is the difference others see in your life because you belong to Christ. Wouldn't it be wonderful if people around you observed, "We can tell he/she has been with Jesus by the way he/she acts and speaks."

Mar 31

Chuckle: *A little boy, doing homework, asked his dad, "Where would I find the Andes?" "Ask your mother," said the dad. "She puts everything away in this house."*

Quote: *"Hail the small sweet courtesies of life, for smooth do they make the road of it." ~ Laurence Sterne*

Courtesy is Contagious

"Get rid of all bitterness, rage, anger, harsh words, and slander, as well as all types of malicious behavior. Instead, be kind to each other, tender-hearted, forgiving one another, just as God through Christ has forgiven you" (Ephesians 4:32 NLT).

The word "courtesy" means friendliness, kindness, politeness in actions and speech, good manners. I like the following by Frank S. Hogan: *"Courteous treatment is a recognition by one person that another person has the same dignity as a human being. The practice of courtesy develops the habit of treating others as equals. It is, therefore, more than a lubricant which prevents irritation between individuals of different backgrounds. It becomes a solvent of the causes of friction and, when constantly applied, produces a positive force in the creation of good will."*

In our modern culture, it seems many people have forgotten the truth of what Publilius Syrus wrote in the first century before the birth of Christ: *"You can accomplish by kindness (courtesy) what you cannot by force."* Being courteous sounds like a small and simple thing for a Christian and should not be difficult to put into practice. Life is full of small grievances which small doses of kindness and courtesy can eliminate.

I've noticed that major disputes between individuals often begin with minor and petty grievances, most of which can be resolved promptly with a small gestures of kindness and courtesy. However, when minor differences are between discourteous people, they can fester and grow into major disputes and become almost impossible to resolve. This is because, over time, the original grievance may fade and the issue can become a personal dislike for one another. Then the participants begin to attack each other rather than dealing with the original grievance.

I'm aware of two Christian men who let an adventuresome cow destroy their friendship and fellowship. A cow belonging to one broke through a fence and ate some delicacies from the garden of the other. Instead of coming together in brotherly love and in a courteous way to resolve the issue, they became angry and bitter and for years they rarely even spoke to one another. How sad. No doubt a show of love, kindness, and courtesy could have resolved the original issue promptly and amicably.

We can make a major contribution to the civility and harmony within our families, churches, and communities if we show the same courtesy to others that we would like to receive.

Apr 01

Chuckle: *A new bride cooked her first meal for her husband. "My mother taught me to cook, and I can cook two things well— apple pie and meatloaf."*

The husband took a bite of his supper and asked, "And which one is this?"

Quote: *"All created things are living in the Hand of God. The senses see only the action of the creatures; but faith sees in everything the action of God." ~ Jean-Pierre de Caussade SJ*

God's Beautiful Creation

"This is what God the LORD says— he who created the heavens and stretched them out, who spread out the earth and all that comes out of it, who gives breath to its people and life to those who walk in it: "I, the LORD, have called you righteous. I will take hold of your hand" (Isaiah 42:5-6 NIV).

Picture with me in your mind's eye, a beautiful crystal-clear mountain stream, Bear Creek, flowing along the base of a 200-feet high cliff on one side and fertile level bottom land on the other. Listen to the gurgling sounds as the water flows over the gravel shoals. Listen to the sounds and smells of mowers cutting hay on the bottom land. As you stand knee-deep in the cool water at the edge of this beautiful stream, casting a lure into the deep blue holes of water, your mind goes back sixty-five years to when you were a teenager and your family lived in this area. You remember playing in this—your favorite— swimming hole. You have always loved this place, but as a teenager you tended to take for granted the pristine beauty of this truly wonderful place.

The above describes what I saw and felt as Dotse and I

visited with my brother and his wife in the beautiful Ozarks of Northwest Arkansas where I grew up. In many ways, it was a true worship experience for me as I relived experiences of long ago. The beauty and complexities of God's creation came rushing anew into my awareness and ignited a new and deeper appreciation for our God and His magnificent creation. We are reminded in Scripture of the message conveyed to us through God's creation. Listen! *"For since the creation of the world God's invisible qualities—his eternal power and divine nature—have been clearly seen, being understood from what has been made, so that men are without excuse"* (Romans 1:20 NIV).

God's general revelation through creation reveals a God of power, intelligence, and intricate detail; a God of order and beauty; a God who controls powerful forces far beyond our ability to fully comprehend. However, it was not until we had the Bible describing the coming of Jesus Christ that we could fully understand God's special revelation of Himself, including the dimensions of His love, grace, and mercy. The Creator of the universe made it possible for us to experience His forgiveness of sin and His promise of eternal life through faith in His Son, Jesus.

Wherever you are today, I encourage you to step back and take a fresh look at God's creation, and marvel at the power, majesty, and handiwork of the God we serve. Also, reflect on Jesus' role in creation. *"Through him (Jesus) all things were made; without him nothing was made that has been made"* (John 1:3 NIV).

Apr 02

Chuckle: *"You know you're getting old when you get the same sensation from a rocking chair that you once got from a roller coaster."*

Quote: *"When you really see Jesus, I defy you to doubt him. When he says 'Do not let your hearts be troubled,' if you see him I defy you to trouble your mind, it is a moral impossibility to doubt when he is there."* ~ Oswald Chambers

Doubters and Cynics

"When doubts filled my mind, your comfort gave me renewed hope and cheer" (Psalm 94:19 NLT).

We all are familiar with the Bible story of "doubting Thomas." After Jesus' had risen from the dead, *". . . the other disciples told him (Thomas), 'We have seen the Lord!' But he said to them, 'Unless I see the nail marks in his hands and put my finger where the nails were, and put my hand into his side, I will not believe it'"* (John 20:25 NIV).

First, let's think about the difference between doubt and cynicism. The doubter is unsure about whether something is true or right, but is open to evidence that his doubt may not be justified. However, the cynic does not believe that people are ever sincere, honest, or good, and tends to be bitter and negative about life. Such a person is not as open to evidence refuting his conclusions and sometimes has the attitude "don't confuse me with the facts, my mind is made up."

"To believe is to be 'in one mind' about accepting something as true; to disbelieve is to be 'in one mind' about rejecting it. To doubt is to waver between the two, to believe and disbelieve at once and so be 'in two minds.' "(Os Guinness, "In Two Minds.")

Jesus never condemned Thomas for having honest doubts. Jesus appeared to Thomas and patiently said to him, *"Put your finger here; see my hands. Reach out your hand and put it into my side. Stop doubting and believe. Thomas said to him, 'My Lord and my God'"* (John 20:27-28 NIV). You see, Thomas was open to being convinced—and stopped short of actually feeling the wounds of Jesus. He became convinced by Jesus' invitation to feel him and immediately voiced his belief.

Some people need to doubt before they can believe. If doubts lead one to ask honest questions, and accept truthful answers, then doubt has been a good thing. But when doubt leads to stubborn cynicism and stubbornness becomes a mind-set, then that cynicism does extreme harm to one's faith.

If you find yourself doubting the truths of the Bible, or God Himself, please don't let your search for truth end there. As you discover answers, let those answers deepen your faith. I believe God would have you bring your doubts directly to Him as you pray. Be honest about your doubts, as Thomas was, and pour out your heart's concerns to the Lord.

Then be open to new insights as He reveals His truths. If you have this attitude, even doubt can serve to bring you closer to Him. God has said, *"I will never fail you. I will never forsake you"* (Hebrews 13:5 NLT). Take God at His word and never doubt His love, His power, His provision, and His promises.

Apr 03

Chuckle: *"As the story goes, Joseph was criticized for loaning the tomb he had worked so hard to carve out. Joseph replied, "But it's only for the weekend."*

Quote: *"If you are too busy to spend time alone with God, you are busier then God intends for you to be."*
~ Unknown Source

Believe and Receive

"When you ask, you must believe (have faith) and not doubt" (James 1:6 NIV). Jesus said, *"... whatever you ask for in prayer, believe (have faith) that you have received it and it will be yours"* (Mark 11:24 NIV).

Think back with me to yesterday. From the time you awoke until you went to bed last night, how many times did you feel inadequate and lacking in wisdom to deal with a situation you were facing? If, after careful reflection on this question, you answer "none," then you probably went through the day depending upon your own strength and wisdom to make decisions and deal with issues that arose. You see, even if we think we know the best answer to a problem, or the best way to handle a situation, we are settling for second best wisdom—ours.

In our first passage James is referring to prayer for wisdom. However, when we ask God for wisdom, or anything, we must believe and not doubt. From our two passages, we see that believing (having faith) is essential for God to answer our prayers and grant our requests. Faith is believing God and acting on that faith. "If God says it, I believe it, and I will ask him!" When you pray, do you do so with confidence that God will answer, or is prayer just one more possibility among other resources you depend upon to handle life situations? Maybe you pray something like this: "OK, Lord, I'm asking, but I don't really think you will answer my prayer." What kind of faith is that? A doubting Christian is one who says he trusts God, but really trusts himself or someone else more. He says he has faith but he really doesn't.

A doubting mind is not convinced that God's way is best. Such a person makes God's Word just like human advice and retains the option to disregard or disobey it. This kind of person vacillates between allegiance to his subjective feelings, the world's ideas, and God's commands. He is divided inside. God's Word says he is "double-minded." *"That person (without faith) should not think he will receive anything from the Lord; he is a double-minded person, unstable in all he does"* (James 1:7-8 NIV).

A double-minded Christian is one who knows Christ as Savior and is going to heaven, but on a daily basis does not have the faith to trust God in all situations and depend upon His divine wisdom to guide his life. We can pray all night to no avail unless we believe God and take Him at His word. *"Without faith, it is impossible to please God"* (Hebrews 11:6 NIV).

A pastor said this, *"True wisdom enables us to do the right thing in the face of moral dilemmas and to interpret life's experiences in light of eternal values."* Only God can grant this true wisdom for living. If we pray with God's will uppermost in our minds, our prayers will be pleasing to Him and we can express our desires to Him with the expectation that He will answer.

Apr 04

Chuckle: *"The odds of an open-faced jelly sandwich landing face down on the floor are directly correlated to the newness, color, and cost of the carpet!!"*

Quote: *"Bitterness imprisons life; love releases it. Bitterness paralyzes life; love empowers it. Bitterness sours life; love heals it. Bitterness blinds life; love anoints its eye."*
~ Harry Emerson Fosdick

Bitterness Can Destroy Us

"See to it that no one misses the grace of God and that no <u>root of bitterness</u> grows up to cause trouble and defile man" (Hebrews 12:15 NIV).

Have you noticed that some people just seem to be angry and bitter by nature? When we see folks in that state of mind, we would do well to consider what may have caused them to be that way. Also, each of us should ask God to help us avoid becoming bitter.

Bitterness has a way of destroying our happiness and our appeal to others. The reasons for bitterness are sometimes difficult to identify and even more difficult to root out. It might be the result of abuse and other deep hurts received as a child—hurts that seem impossible to forget. It might result from hurtful and demeaning remarks from a family member, friend, or co-worker. It might come from being cheated or defrauded in some way. It can come from a sense of being treated unjustly.

Often the person who hurt you in some way is unaware of the extent of your bitterness. If not dealt with in a godly way, time—rather than diminishing the hurt—seems to sharpen the pain and drive the bitterness even deeper into your soul, causing it to fester, grow, and take control of your life. It will cause you to be a pessimist rather than an optimist. It will cause you to see the glass as half empty rather than half full. It will adversely impact your attitude about everything.

Once bitterness reaches a certain level, it becomes easier to justify. You feel so justified in your feelings of anger, hurt, and disappointment that you even become comfortable with those feelings. You become suspicious of the motives of others and read something sinister into everything they do and say in order to feed your feelings of bitterness and self-pity. This type of bitterness can cause people to go for years without speaking or interacting with one another. It can destroy family relationships and even fellowship between church members.

If you are harboring bitterness toward someone, please remember it has the potential to destroy you—your happiness, your influence, and your usefulness to your Lord. Such feelings toward others can interfere with your ability to worship our Lord in a way acceptable to Him.

But the good news is that your anger and bitterness are not outside the reach of God's grace, healing, and forgiveness. I like these words by Henry Blackaby: *"When you allow bitterness to grow in your life, you reject the grace of God that can free you. If you are honest before God, you will admit the bitterness and allow God to forgive you (and heal you). Bitterness enslaves you, but God is prepared to remove your bitterness and replace it with his peace and joy."*

Apr 05

Chuckle: *"A human-resources manager was going over one candidate's application. At the end of the line, 'Sign Here,' the woman had written, 'Pisces.'"* ~ James Dent

Quote: *"The person who is busy counting his blessings has no time to take inventory of his injuries."* ~ William Arthur Ward

Overcoming Bitterness

"See to it that no one misses the grace of God and that no bitter root grows up to cause trouble and defile many" (Hebrews 12:15 NIV). *"Looking carefully lest anyone fall short of the grace of God; lest any root of bitterness springing up cause trouble"* (NKJV).

Here is yet another way of saying the first phrase of this verse: *"Look after each other so that none of you will miss out on the special favor of God"* (NLT). You cannot miss the strong message that each of us should have a special concern for our fellow believers and help them grow in Christ. You can just feel the love, warmness, and oneness among believers that the writer of Hebrews is advocating.

This kind of relationship is based on unconditional love and mutual respect. Such relationships among Christians will be used of God to bless the lives of non-believers and draw them to Christ.

We are also warned about letting bitterness disrupt our relationships. Like a small root that grows into a huge tree, the smallest bitter feeling toward another can grow into a monster that destroys even our most cherished Christian relationships. Such bitterness, if left unchecked, can become so deep-rooted within our souls that it is difficult to weed out. A "bitter root" sometimes comes when we don't get our way; or when we allow disappointment in others to grow into resentment; or when we nurse grudges over past hurts. The fruits of bitterness include jealousy, dissension, and general disharmony in the fellowship.

It's so easy to rationalize and justify our bitterness, especially when we feel we have become the object of unkindness or mistreatment. You may say, "After what that person did to me, I have every right to be bitter." If you are trying to justify your bitterness, beware that if the bitterness is allowed to fester and grow, you can become so used to living with it that it becomes a permanent part of your personality.

You may become comfortable with your bitterness, but no one else will be. Others will be repulsed and driven away. God knows that bitterness will eventually destroy you. He understands the final outcome of uncontrolled bitterness and anger. If you are harboring bitterness, you should understand that there is nothing so deeply imbedded in your heart that God cannot root out and remove. When we allow the indwelling Holy Spirit to take control of our lives, He can heal even the deepest of hurts that result in bitterness.

If you choose to live with bitterness in your heart, you are denying God's grace the opportunity to set you free from these horrible feelings that rob you of your joy. Why not go to God in prayer asking forgiveness for harboring that bitterness in your heart and let Him take it away and replace it with His peace and joy? Then complete your restoration process, by asking forgiveness from the person to whom you are embittered as well.

Apr 06

Chuckle: Sign on an Optometrist's Office: *"If you don't see what you're looking for, you've come to the right place."*

Quote: *"Confidence is contagious. So is lack of confidence."* ~ Michael O'Brien

Living with Confidence

"This is the confidence we have in approaching God: that we ask anything according to his will and he hears us" (I John 5:14 NIV). *"So do not throw away your confidence; it will be richly rewarded. You need to persevere so that when you have done the will of God, you will receive what he has promised"* (Hebrews 10:35-36 NIV).

Have you noticed how some Christians exude confidence and optimism in every circumstance? Nothing seems to get them down. They have an aura of inner peace and contentment about them. Sometimes those who have the most reasons to be depressed and discouraged become blessings to others because they have such confidence in God's ability to sustain them. They inspire others to examine their own faith and dependence upon God. They always have a smile and a positive word no matter how difficult times may be for them. They just have too much going for them.

We can have confidence in approaching God in prayer. *"Let us then approach the throne of grace with confidence, so that we may receive mercy and find grace to help us in our time of need"* (Hebrews 4:16 NIV). As we pray, our confidence grows from knowing our prayers are consistent with God's will. When we align our prayers with His will, He will listen and give us a definite answer. We should pray with confidence!

We can have confidence that God is with us in every circumstance. In our Hebrews 10 passage, we are encouraged not to abandon confidence in our faith in times of disappointments and trials, but rather to show by our endurance that our faith is real. Because of what Christ has done for us, we should have confidence that He will sustain us today and in the future. God has promised never to leave us or forsake us. Such a promise should build our confidence in God's presence, provision, and protection no matter what we face in this life.

We can have confidence that our eternal home is being prepared. Jesus said, *"I am going to prepare a place for you. And if I go and prepare a place for you, I will come again and take you to be with me that you also may be where I am"* (John 14:2b-3 NIV). This is a promise from our Lord Himself for those who have accepted Him as Savior. As believers, we need not fear death.

I once sat by the bedside of a dying, godly aunt. As we talked, she blessed my heart when she said she was not afraid of death. She had accepted the fact that her earthly life was drawing to a close and saw death as a part of life. She was confident that even though she was walking *"through the valley of the shadow of death, she feared no evil, for God was with her"* (Psalm 23:4 NIV).

I pray your confidence in your Lord and His Word will grow, while depending upon the companionship and strength of His Holy Spirit to meet every need in your life.

Apr 07

Chuckle: *A customer said to the salesman, "I want to try on that suit in the window." The salesman replied, "Oh, Sir, we couldn't allow that. You have to use the dressing room like everyone else."*

Quote: *"God loves you because of who God is, not because of anything you did or didn't do."* ~ Regina Brett

The Cost of Following Jesus

Another of his disciples said, "Lord, first let me return home and bury my father." But Jesus told him, "Follow me now! Let those who are spiritually dead care for their own dead" (Matthew 8:21-22 NLT).

The central truth of this passage is that following Jesus will cost you. If you profess to be a Christian and a follower of Christ, but you sacrifice nothing for the relationship with Him, a heart examination is likely long overdue. In our passage, it is possible that the disciple was not asking for permission to go to his father's funeral, but rather to put off following Jesus until a more convenient time—until his elderly father had died.

Jesus never minced words and was always direct with those who expressed a desire to follow Him. He always made certain they weighed the cost of discipleship and their willingness to set aside any personal reservations or conditions which might prevent them from following Him wholeheartedly. Jesus said, *"Anyone who does not take his cross and follow me is not worthy of me"* (Matthew 10:38 NIV).

As God's one and only Son, Jesus did not hesitate to demand complete loyalty and devotion. This means that nothing can be more important to us than our relationship with Him. The decision to follow Jesus should never be put off until a more convenient time. Even when other loyalties and desires compete for our attention, they should never be allowed to become more important than our Lord. If Jesus is your Savior, He also wants to be Lord and Master of your life.

Many "Christians" claim the lordship of Christ in their lives, but at the same time, sin against Him by disobedience and letting sinful lifestyles prevent them from being fully devoted followers of Christ. When we intentionally disobey God's Word, refuse to give up sinful practices, or let other priorities in life take precedence over our relationship with Him, it calls into question our very salvation experience. For a Christian, it is not enough to talk the talk, but we must walk the walk. *"If anyone is in Christ, he is a new creation; the old has gone, and the new has come"* (2 Corinthians 5:17 NIV).

At the beginning, I said following Jesus will cost you something. But let me add, it will not cost you anything worthwhile when compared to the rewards of joy, peace, and contentment that come to fully devoted followers of Christ. Once we surrender completely to Him, everything that was once so important becomes abhorrent to us. The apostle Paul writes, *"Yes, everything else is worthless when compared to the priceless gain of knowing Christ Jesus my Lord. I have discarded everything else, counting it all garbage, so that I may have Christ and become one with him . . ."* (Philippians 3:8 NLT).

Apr 08

Chuckle: *After church one Sunday, a young boy said to his mother, "Mom, I've decided I want to be a minister when I grow up."*

"That's great," said the Mom, "But what made you decide to be a minister?"

"Well," the boy replied, "I'll have to go to church on Sunday anyway, and I figure it will be more fun to stand up and yell than to sit and listen."

Quote: *"It is a brave act of valour to despise death, but where life is more terrifying than death it is then the truest valour to dare to stay alive."* ~ Sir Thomas Browne

Courageous Christian Living

"I command you—be strong and courageous! Do not be afraid or discouraged. For the Lord your God is with you wherever you go" (Joshua 1:9 NLT).

J. Edger Hoover described courage this way: *"It is a priceless ingredient of character. The will to do, the tenacity to overcome all obstacles and finish the course, the strength to cling to inexorable ideals are rooted in courage. It is the outward manifestation of our spiritual development."*

We all admire those who display unusual courage and bravery in the face of danger and/or adversity. Courage is a quality of the mind, and as such, it ranks among the cardinal virtues. It's opposite—cowardice—ranks among the most serious character flaws. Like the wind, courage can only be seen by its manifestations. We can't see the wind but are well aware of its effects. We know a person has courage not by his looks or words, but by observing his actions. Courage is not only a Christian duty but a constant for the person who, without reservations, places himself in the hands of God. Courage becomes evident in patient endurance, moral purity, spiritual maturity, and fidelity.

The Scriptures are replete with admonitions for us to be courageous, to stand firm, to be strong, and to depend upon God to provide the strength to endure even in the most difficult of circumstances. The kind of courage God desires motivates us to reach the world for Christ and minister to those in need. Courage gives us the mental, emotional, and spiritual toughness that enables us to stand by our convictions and the necessary strength to build and sustain a free and moral society and nation. It allows us to face the perpetrators of the most heinous evil acts with confidence and moral fortitude.

Godly courage will allow us to stand by our convictions, discern right from wrong, and uphold that which is right in the eyes of God. Listen to the apostle Paul: *"Therefore, my dear brothers, stand firm. Let nothing move you. Always give yourselves fully to the work of the Lord, because you know that your labor in the Lord is not in vain"* (1 Corinthians 15:58 NIV). *"Be on your guard; stand firm in the faith; be men of courage; be strong. Do everything in love"* (1 Corinthians 16:13 NIV). *"He that loses wealth loses much: But he that loses courage loses all."* ~ Cervantes

Apr 09

Chuckle: *"Have you ever wondered why Goofy stands erect while Pluto remains on all fours? They're both dogs!"*

Quote: *"Jesus will not overlook your shortcomings or simply encourage you to do better the next time. He will give you victory in the midst of your failure."* ~ Henry Blackaby

A "Crutch" For the Weak

"Therefore I will boast all the more gladly about my weaknesses, so that Christ's power may rest on me. . . . For when I am weak, then I am strong" (2 Corinthians 12:9b, 10b NIV).

I once read about a controversial celebrity who said that religion/Christianity was only a "crutch" for the weak. He meant this statement to be a put-down of Christians whom he saw as only a bunch of insecure people who cling to religion out of desperation—too weak to stand on their own. Without realizing it, he had expressed an eternal truth about the relationship of Christians to their Lord. He was exactly right about our dependence upon God, but our Lord is so much more than a crutch. He is:

- Our Savior because we cannot save ourselves;
- Our lifeboat in a sea of despair;
- Our shield protecting us from the evil one;
- Our strength in our times of greatest weakness;
- Our companion when we are lonely;
- Our comfort when we are grieving;
- Our peace in the storms of life;
- Our "Crutch" to help us walk with Him;
- Our . . . . You fill in the blank.

So it is perfectly accurate to say Christianity is a crutch for the weak. "Crutch" is not the best word, but it communicates our need for God. The problem with most of us is that our pride will not allow us to see ourselves as weak and in need of a God's help. We must learn to see ourselves as God sees us. He recognizes our weaknesses and our desperate need for His strength every day.

I once knew a youth minister who signed all his correspondence with, "Striving to be weak." This young man had come to understand that God is His strongest when we are our weakest—that in our weakness, God's power is made manifest through us. It is a sign of courage and humility when a person comes to realize his dependence upon God. He recognizes that his strength is totally inadequate to solve the problems facing him.

When we consider that God's power is displayed in proportion to our weakness, we should be encouraged and our hope should be increased. The critical factor in this equation is whether or not we recognize our weaknesses and limitations. It's only when we acknowledge our weaknesses that we will learn to depend upon God instead of our own abilities, strength, and energy. When we affirm God's strength and our weakness, He will develop our character and deepen our worship.

Apr 10

Chuckle: *A boy served morning coffee to his grandmother. When finished, she asked, "why are there three little toy Army guys in the bottom of my cup."*

The grandson replied, "You know, Grammy, it's like on TV. The best part of waking up is soldiers in your cup."

Quote: *"Light that makes some things seen, makes some things invisible. Were it not for darkness and the shadow of the earth, the noblest part of the Creation would remain unseen, and the stars in heaven invisible."* ~ Sir Thomas Brown, Adapted

From Darkness to Light

"In him (Jesus) was life, and that life was the light of men. The light shines in the darkness, but the darkness has not understood it. There came a man who was sent from God; his name was John. He came as a witness to testify concerning that light, so that through him all men might believe . . . The true light that gives light to every man was coming into the world" (John 1:4-9 NIV).

In the Scriptures, God has much to say about darkness and light. They are metaphors used to describe the ruler of darkness and evil (Satan) versus the Light of the World (Jesus) and the righteousness of God.

You will remember the account in Genesis 1:3 when God said, *"Let there be light,"* and there was light. The first time God said, "Let there be light," He illuminated our physical world with the sun and reflective moon. The second time God said, "Let there be light," He sent His Son—the Light of the World— to illuminate the hearts and minds of people where the darkness of sin had taken root.

As I pondered the above quote, the phrases reminded me that the Light of the World illuminates the darkness of our sins and makes them visible to us by the convicting power of His Holy Spirit. That same Light renders our confessed and forgiven sins invisible—even to God Himself. Our sins are blotted out by the blood of Jesus. It is as if those sins had never occurred. We are told that God remembers our sins no more (Hebrews 8:12) when we repent of our sins and pray to receive Jesus Christ as Savior and Lord. We are *"a people belonging to God . . . who called you out of darkness into his wonderful light"* (1 Peter 2:9 NIV).

Like the stars which shine their brightest in the darkest of night, the Light of the World shines His brightest in the darkness of a sinful world. The darkness we once experienced allows us to see more clearly and experience the brightness, beauty, and benevolence of God's redeeming love and light. If you allow Christ to guide your life, you will never need to stumble into the darkness of sin again. *"In Him there is no darkness at all"* (1 John 1:5 NIV).

An old hymn: *"The whole world was lost in the darkness of sin, The Light of the world is Jesus; Like sunshine at noon-day His glory shone in, The Light of the world is Jesus."*

Apr 11

Chuckle: Child's comment on marriage: *"No person really decides before they grow up who they're going to marry. God decides it all way before, and you get to find out later who you're stuck with."* ~ Kristen, age 10

Quote: *"Among the things you can give and still keep are your word, a smile, and a grateful heart."* ~ Zig Ziglar

The Door to Your Heart

"Look! Here I stand at the door (of your heart) and knock. If you hear me calling and open the door, I will come in, and we will share a meal as friends" (Revelation 3:20 NLT).

Our passage is from a letter from Jesus to the church at Laodicea. This was a church that had become comfortable with the status quo. It was wealthy and lacked for nothing, but had lost its vision for what a New Testament church should be. The people had become complacent and self-centered. Jesus accused them of being "lukewarm" and disgusting to Him. He said He was going to "spew" them out of His mouth because they were neither hot nor cold. Christ was showing the Laodiceans that true value is not in material possessions, but in a right relationship with God.

Our desire for money, pleasure, and material possessions can be dangerous because their temporary satisfaction can cause us to be indifferent to God's offer of lasting fulfilment and happiness. In reality, our possessions and achievements are worthless when compared with the everlasting future of Christ's Kingdom.

But Jesus had not given up on the Laodiceans, and neither has He given up on us. If your relationship with our Lord has become lukewarm, He wants you to repent and return to Him.

In our passage, Jesus is standing at the door of our "lukewarm" hearts. He is knocking on our heart's door and calling out for us to open the door. But if we are doing our own things behind the locked door of our turned away hearts, we will no longer hear God because we are too busy disobeying the greatest commandment: *"Love the Lord our God with all your heart and with all your soul and with all your mind and with all your strength"* (Mark 12:30 NIV).

If our hearts are turned away from God, we do not want to hear God. We want to do our own thing. Notice that Jesus didn't assume that He would be heard. He said, "<u>if</u> anyone hears my voice." We can easily get so far away from God that we can no longer hear His voice.

Notice that Jesus does not break down the door to our hearts, but gently, lovingly knocks and calls out for our attention. He allows us to decide whether or not we will listen to His call and open the door.

Have you found yourself deliberately and intentionally keeping Christ's life-changing presence and power on the other side of the firmly locked door of your heart? If so, you would do well to open your heart to Him in an attitude of repentance and let Him restore your joy. Say to God: I'm wrong, I'm sorry, please forgive me, cleanse me, empower me anew with your Spirit, and use me once again as your vessel for your glory!

Apr 12

Chuckle: *A man was looking at himself in a mirror. He said, "I look horrible, I feel fat and ugly. Please pay be a compliment." The wife said, "Your eyesight is near perfect!"*

Quote: *"Spiritual growth involves a constantly changing conception of a changeless God."* ~ William Arthur Ward

It Runs in the Family

"Whoever does God's will is my brother and sister and mother" (Mark 3:35 NLT).

From time to time I call my son at his workplace. The person answering the phone often says my voice and my son's sound exactly the same. His voice sounds like his Father's voice. How often have you observed that someone walks, talks, acts, or looks like his or her parents? We call these characteristics family traits, and we sometimes hear words like, "it runs in the family."

In our passage, Jesus says if we do the will of God, we are His family. Also, in Ephesians 2:19, we are told that we are *"members of God's household."* If we are members of His family, our lives will reflect the traits of Jesus—we will become like Him. People will be reminded of Him when they see or hear us. I'm reminded of the words of the apostle Paul, *"Your attitude (mind) should be the same as that of Christ Jesus"* (Philippians 2:5 NIV). Of course, it is our attitude/mind that determines how we talk and act. It is God's will that we become more and more like Jesus each day and exhibit the family traits that we see in Him.

When Jesus was here on earth, He walked daily in close communion with and submission to His Father. When we do the same things, we share a family trait with Jesus as His brothers and sisters. The Bible tells us that we should *"be imitators of God, therefore, as dearly loved children and live a life of love, just as Christ loved us and gave himself up for us as a fragrant offering and sacrifice to God"* (Ephesians 5:1-2 NIV).

Just as children imitate their parents who love them, it should be our desire to imitate our Lord. His great love caused Him to sacrifice Himself for you and me so that we might live. Our love for others should be just like Jesus' love for us—a love that goes far beyond affection to self-sacrificing service. This kind of love should be a spiritual family trait in the family of Christ. It should run in our family. *"Therefore, as we have opportunity, let us do good to all people, especially to those who belong to the family of believers"* (Galatians 6:10 NIV).

Apr 13

Chuckle: *"Mom, there's a man at the door collecting for the Old Folks Home. Shall I give him Grandma?"*

Quote: *"Happy families are all alike; every unhappy one is unhappy in its own way."* ~ Leo Tolstoy

Family: Our Treasure

"How happy are those who fear the LORD—all who follow his ways! You will enjoy the fruit of your labor. How happy you will be! How rich your life! Your wife will be like a fruitful vine, flourishing in your home. And look at all those children! There they sit around your table as vigorous and healthy as young olive trees. That is the LORD's reward for those who fear him. . . May you live to enjoy your grandchildren" (Psalm 128:1-4, 6 NLT).

As I grow older, my family members become more and more precious to me—both my extended family as well as my immediate family. A few weekends back some members of our family—my wife's lineage—came together to enjoy a time of fun, food, and fellowship. Some had not seen each other in many years. It was a wonderful time of getting reacquainted, sharing life's experiences, recalling precious memories, and strengthening the bonds of love between us. From this experience came a desire to make the get-together an annual event, and to make every effort to include even more family members next time.

In our society, family members are often scattered over great distances and it is increasingly difficult, if not impossible, to bring all of them together—except perhaps for funerals. As I conduct funeral services, I often remind family members that life is brief and they should never pass up an opportunity to come together and express their love for one another. Failure to do so can bring lingering feelings of guilt and regret after a loved one passes away.

We know it is God's plan that the family be the building block for society. He instituted the family in creation and even saved Noah's family unit when He destroyed life on the earth with the great flood. Strong, godly families make strong churches, communities, and nations. I think we all agree that the rapid disintegration of the family in our society contributes to all sorts of social ills. As Christians, we should be faithful to heal and protect our family relationships in ways that bless one another and honor God.

Family fulfils the human need for love, companionship, and procreation. It is also the setting within which our religious faith is nurtured through the examples and teachings of parents and other relatives. Family relationships do not remain warm and close automatically. They must be nurtured through love, communication, family worship, conflict resolution, and even healthy friendships outside the family.

I hope you see your family members as your greatest treasure, and I encourage you to never pass up an opportunity to let each one of them know how much you love and appreciate them. We never know when we will do so for the very last time.

Apr 14

Chuckle: *A Sunday School teacher: "Now children, never do anything in private you wouldn't do in public."*

"Hurrah!" shouted one little boy—"No more baths!"

Quote: *"We must learn to live together as brothers or perish together as fools."* ~ Martin Luther King, Jr

Favoritism Is Sinful

"For God does not show favoritism" (Romans 2:11 NIV). *"My dear brothers and sisters, how can you claim that you have faith in our glorious Lord Jesus Christ if you favor some people more than others"* (James 2:1 NLT). *"But if you show favoritism, you sin and are convicted by the law as lawbreakers"* (James 2:9 NIV).

Favoritism means to receive or reject someone based on appearance or other imposed standards. However, favoritism defines a person in terms apart from God's grace. James zeros in on favoritism, partiality, prejudice, and snobbery. These attitudes lead to discrimination against certain people whom we are uncomfortable being around. James reminds us that if we show favoritism to some at the expense of others, we sin.

We know that Jesus loves everyone equally, but gave special attention to the poor, the sick, and the powerless—the ones we often reject. We should follow His lead. *"I now realize how true it is that God does not show favoritism but accepts men from every nation who fear him and do what is right"* (Acts 10:34 NIV).

We may have favorites based on such things as appearance, age, affluence, or ancestry. If we could only grasp the eternal truth that God made every one of us and we are all the same in His sight, it would change our whole view of life, and give us the ability to love and accept everyone without reservation.

"Mohandas K. (Mahatma) Gandhi was the leader of the Indian nationalist movement against British rule and considered the father of his country. He is internationally esteemed for his doctrine of nonviolence to achieve political and social progress. Gandhi says in his autobiography that in his student days he was truly interested in the Bible. Deeply touched by reading the Gospels, he seriously considered becoming a convert, since Christianity seemed to offer the real solution to the caste system that was dividing the people of India. One Sunday, he went to a nearby church to attend services. He decided to see the minister and ask for instruction in the way of salvation and enlightenment on other doctrines. But when he entered the sanctuary, the ushers refused to give him a seat and suggested that he go and worship with his own people. Gandhi left and never came back. 'If Christians have caste differences also,' he said to himself, 'I might as well remain a Hindu.'" ~ Illustrations for Biblical Preaching; Edited by Michael P. Green

In our key passage, James questions our faith if we favor some over others. We must have the attitude of Christ and welcome everyone into our fellowship equally (see Philippians 2:5). We should say, "Your appearance, race, nationality, ethnic background, or social status, doesn't matter. You are loved and welcomed in this fellowship.

Apr 15

Chuckle: *While bragging about their dads, the first boy said, "My dad scribbled a few words on a piece of paper, called it a poem, and they gave him $50."*

The second boy said, "That's nothing. My dad scribbled a few words on a piece of paper, called it a song, and they gave him $100."

The third boy said, "I got you both beat. My dad scribbled a few words on a piece of paper, called it a sermon, and it took eight people to collect all the money."

Quote: *"So long as we love, we serve; so long as we are loved by others, I should say that we are almost indispensable; and no man is useless while he has a friend."* ~ Robert Louis Stevenson

Valued Friendships

Jesus said to His disciples: *"I command you to love one another in the same way that I love you"* (John 15:12 NLT). *"The greatest love is shown when people lay down their lives for their friends"* (John 15:13b NLT).

I'm sure each of us has a personal definition of a true friend that has evolved from our own experiences in human relationships. Someone has defined a true friend as *"the first person who comes in when the whole world has gone out."* Someone else has said, *"Value a friend who, for you, finds time on his calendar—but cherish the friend who, for you, does not even consult his calendar."* Today, let's consider this question: Am I the friend that is cherished by those who call me friend?

Hopefully, we will not be required to give our lives for our friends, but there are numerous other ways to show the nature of our love and friendship to our brothers and sisters in Christ.

Our sacrificial love can be shown by helping, listening, encouraging, and giving. I think Jesus is saying that we should search out those who need this kind of love and do everything possible to meet that need—then give even more of ourselves. True friends always place the needs of friends ahead of their own. They live for others rather than themselves.

Casual acquaintances will not suffice as substitutes for genuine friends. However, I think many of us live in a world of acquaintances rather than unwavering friends. Acquaintances may fool us into thinking they are friends, but "a false friend is like your shadow. As long as there is sunshine, he sticks close by, but the minute you step into the shade, he disappears." We have not truly lived until we have a wall of love and friendship surrounding us to protect us from storms of life.

"Oh, the comfort, the inexpressible comfort, of feeling safe with a person, having neither to weigh thoughts nor measure words, but to pour them all out just as they are, chaff, grain together, knowing that a faithful hand will take and sift them, keeping what is worth keeping, and then, with a breath of kindness blow the rest away." ~ George Eliot

Apr 16

Chuckle: *"I drive much too fast to worry about cholesterol"*
Quote: *"My best friend is the one who brings out the best in me."* ~ Henry Ford

Lasting Friendships

"There are 'friends' who destroy each other, but a real friend sticks closer than a brother" (Proverbs 18:24 NLT).

It's easy to treat people as a means to an end rather than as ends in themselves. As a gregarious man once boasted, 'I have friends I haven't used yet.' A false friend is like your shadow. As long as there is sunshine, he sticks close by. But the minute you step into the shade, he disappears.

Do you have someone who you consider a close friend? Is that person trustworthy with even your most personal information? Is that person someone who lifts you up with wise and helpful counsel when appropriate? In our selfish, what's-in-it-for-me, world, it seems to me that true, genuine, lasting friendships are few and far between. In many situations, casual acquaintances have been substituted for legitimate friendships. Many people are lonely among the crowds and feel cut off and alienated from other people. When they look at all the people around them, it makes them even more aware of their isolation. As we think about friendships today, let's do so from two perspectives: the friend you need, and the friend you are.

We all need of friends who genuinely care about us, stick close to us, listen to us, and offer loving assistance when needed. A true friend is not judgmental, but offers love, encouragement, support, unselfish advice, and constructive criticism when appropriate. It is better to have one friend like this than dozens of false and superficial "friends." A true friend is not hot and cold—he or she is consistent and always has your best interests at heart. *"A friend loves at all times, and a brother is born for adversity"* (Proverbs 17:17 NIV).

A friend who genuinely cares about you may find it necessary to give you unpleasant counsel and advice at times. However, you will always know that such advice from a trusted friend is for your own good. *"Wounds from a friend are better than many kisses from an enemy"* (Proverbs 27:6 NLT). On the other hand, a false friend may whisper soothing and sweet words; and happily send you on your way. Even though painful at times, a friend's advice can be very beneficial if we will only listen. *"The heartfelt counsel of a friend is as sweet as perfume and incense"* (Proverbs 27:9 NLT).

The best way to find a true friend is to be one. There are people around you who are in desperate need of a friend. Ask God to guide you to a person with a friendship need that only you can satisfy, then accept the challenge of being a true and trusted friend. Be aware that a careless tongue will destroy trust, the very foundation of friendships. *"A troublemaker plants seeds of strife; a gossip separates the best of friends"* (Proverbs 16:28 NLT). An extension and paraphrase of the Golden Rule: Be a friend.

Apr 17

Chuckle: *"Laffing iz the sensation ov pheeling good all over, and showing it principally in one spot."* ~ Josh Billings

Quote: *"Many persons have a wrong idea of what constitutes real happiness. It is not obtained through self-gratification, but through fidelity to a worthy purpose."* ~ Helen Keller

Having Fun Yet?

Jesus said, *"My purpose is to give life in all its fullness"* (John 10:10 NIV).

Having fun is one of the greatest blessings of life, and I believe God created us to be happy, to laugh, and have fun. As we think about having fun in this life, let's begin by defining "fun." What is fun anyway? Before you go looking in the dictionary, try to define "fun" from your own experiences. I suspect your definition contains words like: play, enjoyment, happiness, laughter, amusement, good times, etc. Now, which of these words describing "fun" <u>does God not want us to have</u> as Christians? I believe the *"life in all its fullness"* that Jesus promises in our text will be a life filled with fun. If I were to select a synonym for "fun", it would be rejoicing or happiness.

When we are happy and having fun, we will *"Always be full of joy in the Lord. I say it again—rejoice!"* (Philippians 4:4 NLT). Paul was in prison when he penned these encouraging words to the church at Philippi. In other words, he did not allow his adverse circumstances to spoil his inner attitude of happiness, and he wanted the Christians at Philippi to share in his unspeakable joy because of his relationship to his Lord. This line of thinking reminds me of a book we have entitled: "Happiness is a choice." We can be happy and have fun if we decide to do so. *"This is the day the Lord has made. We will rejoice and be glad in it"* (Psalm 118:24 NLT).

Each day, without really trying, we can find reasons to be down in the dumps and miserable in our self-pity. But this is not God's plan for your life. Because of His indescribable love, amazing grace, and limitless mercy, we always have reason to rejoice, be happy, and have fun. Life can be a "hoot" if we retain our sense of humor and determination to be happy. This can happen if you allow God's Holy Spirit to give you an attitude adjustment. He will give you reason to rejoice and enjoy life even in the most adverse circumstances. *"Consider it pure joy, my brothers, whenever you face trials of many kinds"* (James 1:2 NIV).

Finally, no Christian should ever see sinful actions as fun. *"Do not love the world or anything in the world. If anyone loves the world, the love of the Father is not in him"* (1 John 2:15 NIV). "Fun" to a Christian describes those wholesome actions that please God and bring us joy and pleasure. Of course, Satan will try to convince us that sinful behavior is more fun. But we should shun even the very appearance of evil, cling to that which is good, and have fun doing it. *"Hate what is evil; cling to what is good"* (Romans 12:9b NIV). Our greatest joy comes from our relationship with Jesus Christ.

Apr 18

Chuckle: *"Doctor,"* whined the patient, *"I keep seeing spots before my eyes."*

"Why have you come to me? Have you seen an ophthalmologist?"

"No," replied the patient, *"just these spots."*

Quote: *"The person who does things that count doesn't usually stop to count them."* ~ Unknown Source

A Gentle Heart

"Be completely humble and gentle; be patient, bearing with one another in love" (Ephesians 4:2 NIV).

In Galatians 5:22, we find the fruits of the Spirit recorded. They are the products of Christ's control of our lives by His Spirit within us. They include love, joy, peace, patience, kindness, goodness, faithfulness, gentleness, and self-control. Notice that "gentleness" is one of the indicators of a Holy Spirit filled and controlled life.

The word "gentleness" suggests the yielding of a judge, who, instead of demanding the exact penalty required by strict justice, gives way to circumstances which call for leniency and mercy. The word also suggests mildness of manner; or easy, not rough or harsh, in dealing with others. It is closely related to "kindness." It certainly should be one of the Christ-like qualities of every believer. A gentle person is one to whom we are readily attracted—one who we are comfortable being around.

As Christians we are privileged that God has chosen us to be Christ's representatives here on earth. *"We are therefore Christ's ambassadors, as though God were making his appeal through us"* (2 Corinthians 5:20 NIV). As such, we are challenged each day to live worthy of the calling we have received. We are to *"gently instruct, in the hope that God will grant them repentance leading them to a knowledge of the truth"* (2 Timothy 2:25 NIV). When we think about how gentle, patient, and loving God has been with us, we should be adequately motivated to let His attributes flow through us.

The very nature of God is revealed through the life of a gentle person. We can be sure that others are watching those of us who claim the name of Christ to see if we are genuine—if we practice what we preach. To be genuine, we must know Christ, love Him, remember Him, and imitate Him. *"Live a life filled with love for others, following the example of Christ, who loved you and gave himself as a sacrifice to take away your sins"* (Ephesians 5:2 NLT).

Each day, you and I can be gentle reminders of God's love, grace, mercy, and gentleness. Let's join our hearts in prayer that God will make us gentle and humble in the power of His Holy Spirit.

Apr 19

Chuckle: *One Easter Sunday morning a preacher held up an egg and asked the children, "What's in here?"*
"I know!" a little boy exclaimed. "Pantyhose!"
Quote: *"The sun, which has all those planets revolving around it and dependent upon it, can ripen a bunch of grapes as if it had nothing else in the world to do."* ~ Galileo

God or Nothing

"In the beginning God created the heavens and the earth . . . God saw all that he had made, and it was very good . . ." (Genesis 1:1, 33 NIV).

Galileo (1564-1642), was a pioneer of modern physics and telescopic astronomy. A spacecraft, named for Galileo, was launched from a space shuttle on October 18, 1989 to orbit the planet Jupiter. Many years ago, Alfred Noyes made the following comments in reference to today's quote from Galileo.
"This was Galileo's answer to those who attacked him when he said that the earth was not the center of the universe. His system, the critics said, made human beings insignificant. Galileo's answer, made three hundred years ago, is a source of strength in our time. For today many of us again feel that the individual is insignificant in the immense universe of modern science. But if the physical sun can be so responsible for the minutest flower in the field, there is certainly no reason to feel that there is any limit to the scope of the central Power, God, which created all the suns, all life, all spiritual values and the spirit of man himself. Behind Galileo's defence was his own belief that the universe is centered on neither the earth nor the sun—it is centered on either God or nothing. If the latter, there can be no

real belief, no sense of philosophy. Out of this blind alley, he turns naturally to the other alternative—God. Galileo's words, the first voice of modern science, call us back to faith, hope and true belief."

In our day, there is a constant battle between creationism and evolutionism; between intelligent design and science, with the "big bang" theory thrown in for good measure. In this brief space, I cannot begin to address all the aspects of this ongoing debate, even if I had the understanding to do so. But as I read the words of Galileo, and a discussion of his conclusions, I was reminded once again of the central truth of the universe. God, in all His power and majesty, created all there is and yet is still mindful of each of us. *"What is man that you are mindful of him"* (Hebrews 2:6b). God wants to nurture each human life as the sun nurtures the bunches of grapes and flowers of the field for His glory.

Because of His great love, that nurture has as its first goal to reconcile each person to Himself—to make us acceptable in His sight and presence—through faith in His One and Only Son who was sacrificed for our sins. Then His nurture includes maturing each Christian into a beautiful, blooming, and productive life. He does this through His Word, and the indwelling of His Holy Spirit in a similar way as the rays of the sun nurture each living thing on earth. He wants His Son to be to you what His sun is to a bunch of grapes or a beautiful rose in your yard—as Galileo put it, *"as if He has nothing else in the world to do"* but tend to you. . . .

Apr 20

Chuckle: *On the way home from Sunday morning worship, I said to my wife, "You know, I don't think I have ever preached worse."*

In an effort to cheer me up, she said, "Sure you have, honey."

Quote: *"Take all the pleasures of all the spheres, And multiply each through endless years—One minute of heaven is worth them all."* ~ Thomas Moore

Heaven: Who Will Be There?

"Whoever believes in the Son has eternal life, but whoever rejects the Son will not see life, for God's wrath remains on him" (John 3:36 NIV).

There is a popular belief today that a loving God will allow everyone into heaven as long as there is a thread of decency in their character. It seems that nearly everyone is going to heaven, and hell is reserved for only the vilest of characters like child-molesters, murderers, or other heinous persons that we just don't like. It's understandable that we are repulsed by the thought of a fellow human being spending eternity separated from God in a horrible place the Bible calls hell—a place many say does not exist.

According to Scripture, both heaven and hell are indisputable realities, regardless of our personal feelings about them. Heaven is described as a blissful place of eternal peace, joy, and comfort in the presence of our Lord. R. G. Lee said this about heaven, *"Heaven is the most beautiful place the mind of God could conceive and the hand of God could create."* It is reserved for those who have trusted in Jesus Christ as Savior and Lord as evidenced by their service to Him and other people.

Hell, on the other hand, was not prepared for human beings but for the Devil and his angels. *"Then he will say to those on his left, 'Depart from me, you who are cursed, into the eternal fire prepared for the devil and his angels'"* (Matthew 25:41 NIV). God does not send people to hell; they go there by choice.

We cannot dismiss the reality of hell without dismissing the teachings of Jesus Himself. Jesus was rejected and insulted when He confronted people with the harsh reality of their sins. He often spoke about hell as the place of eternal suffering for those who willfully and persistently reject His love and free gift of salvation by grace through faith in Him.

Yes, hell is a real place that will be inhabited by the eternal souls of real people—even good moral people who have rejected Christ. This truth should never be sugar-coated, glossed over, or watered down to please those who do not want to hear about or acknowledge hell's existence.

So, back to our original question: "Who will go to heaven?" Answer: Those who have humbled themselves before God, repented of their sins, and have received forgiveness by placing their faith in Jesus Christ and His atoning death on Calvary's cross. These words are not Jerry Stratton's opinion but the Words of God Himself as expressed by Jesus Christ and others in the Bible, God's Holy Word.

Apr 21

Chuckle: *"To keep your marriage brimming with love in the loving cup, Whenever you're wrong, admit it. Whenever you are right, shut up."* ~ Ogden Nash

Quote: *"Blessed is the person who is too busy to worry in the daytime and too sleepy to worry at night."* ~ Unknown Source

To Worry Is Wrong

"Do not worry about your life, what you will eat or drink; or about your body, what you will wear" (Matthew 6:25 NIV). *"Seek first his (God's) kingdom and his righteousness, and all these things will be given to you as well. Therefore do not worry about tomorrow, for tomorrow will worry about itself. Each day has enough trouble of its own"* (Matthew 6:33-34 NIV). *"Who of you by worrying can add a single hour to his life?"* (Matthew 6:27 NIV).

From His discourse to His followers in the Sermon on the Mount, Jesus gives us instructions in the practical aspects of Christian living. He deals with a subject here that is very real to many of us—worry. I must admit I've done some major league worrying myself at times. Some people worry about everything as if their worrying will somehow make the dreaded situation more pleasant and acceptable. In reality, worrying about something will not change it one iota. *"Worry is like a rocking chair; it will give you something to do, but it won't get you anywhere."*

Jesus dealt with worry in a straight forward way. He says, *"Do not worry."* He says we are to focus our attention on Him, His kingdom, and His righteousness; then He will provide to us all the needs of life. Most of the time, worrying comes from a feeling of inadequacy to control a situation or solve problems in our lives rather than trusting them to God. When He tells us not to worry but we do it anyway, we are being disobedient and untrusting. We are saying to God, "I don't believe your promise to look after the practical needs of my life, so I must do it myself."

Usually it is the little cares and worries that make us so uncomfortable. Most of the things we worry about either don't materialize or are not nearly as bad as we imagined. If we are worrying, we are not trusting God to deal with the future we cannot see. The only cure for this lack of trust is obedience to His words. *"Now faith is being sure of what we hope for and certain of what we do not see . . . Without faith it is impossible to please God"* (Hebrews 11:1, 6 NIV).

The operative concept here is to abandon yourself into God's hands and trust Him completely. But does this mean we just sit on our hands and do nothing while trusting God to take care of us and grant each little desire of our hearts? Of course not.

He gave us our minds and abilities and we are to use them, for His glory, in providing for our families and ourselves. However, while we are doing our best with talents God has given us, we should not worry. We trust the outcome to God. This allows us to live in peace and contentment rather than anxiety and worry.

Apr 22

Chuckle: *"Since it's the early worm that gets eaten by the bird, sleep late."*

Quote: *"Our worth comes from the image of God in all of us, and must be the basis for our concept of ourselves."*
~ Unknown Source

Your Importance to God

"When I look at the night sky and see the work of Your fingers—, the moon and the stars which You have set in place—what are mortals that you should think of us, mere humans that you should care for us?" (Psalm 8:3-4 NLT).

Each of us was created with a powerful curiosity and the insatiable need to explore God's creation—to go where we've never gone before. We want to know what's beyond that next mountain, ocean, or planet. We may go to new places physically or explore them through written and pictorial descriptions.

Knowing how He had made us, God laid open to us the entire universe to reveal Himself and His power to satisfy our desire for discovery. The more mysteries that are uncovered, the more we find out about who God is and what His attributes are. All His creation helps us to understand not only who God is, but equally important, who God is not. The Bible says He is not limited in power. He is not apathetic about what happens to us. He is not partial. His love is not limited.

We have great worth to God because we bear the stamp of the Creator Himself (see Genesis 1:26a). Great effort is being exerted by scientists to prove any theory other than the miracle of creation by God's own hands. As more scientific evidence is found, it becomes more and more difficult for the non-creationists to explain how the universe and the living creatures therein came into existence. The Scriptures tell us that man has exchanged the truth for a lie.

Paul writes, *"For since the creation of the world God's invisible qualities—his eternal power and divine nature—have been clearly seen, being understood from what has been made, so that men are without excuse. . . Although they claimed to be wise, they became fools and exchanged the glory of the immortal God for images made to look like mortal man and birds and animals and reptiles"* (Romans 1:20, 22-23 NIV).

Yes, God wants us to discover the greatness of His creation which reveals the dimensions of His power and His great love for mankind—the crown of His creation. God has proven over and over how much He loves you and me, with the ultimate expression of His love being shown on a cross outside Jerusalem where His only Son suffered, bled, and died. *"But God demonstrates his own love for us in this: While we were still sinners, Christ died for us"* (Romans 5:8 NIV). How can you read this verse and not see how important you are to God, our Heavenly Father?

God gave us His whole creation to show us the dimensions of His power, and He gave His Son to show us the dimensions of His love. Because God has declared your value to Him, you can be set free from feelings of worthlessness.

Apr 23

Chuckle: *"It is bad to suppress laughter; it goes back down and spreads to your hips."*

Quote: *"A Christian who says he worships God every Sunday morning on the golf course is really worshiping golf on God's course."* ~ Unknown Source

Why Attend Church?

"Think of ways to encourage one another by outbursts of love and good deeds. And let us not neglect our meeting together, as some people do, but encourage and warn each other, especially now that the day of his coming back again is drawing near" (Hebrews 10:24-25 NLT).

I've often heard someone say, "I'm a Christian and have a close relationship with the Lord, but I can worship him without attending church." Of course we can worship God any time, but it is God's plan that we should assemble ourselves regularly for corporate worship and fellowship. No doubt our primary reason for assembling in God's house is to meet Him, as a body of believers, and worship Him through confession, repentance, praise, prayer, and thanksgiving. However, there are other benefits from worshiping together. Relationships are strengthened, fellowship becomes warmer, and mutual encouragement becomes a powerful force in our lives.

As the day when Christ will return draws closer, we see opposition to Christianity growing, even in our own country. Persecution of Christians is on the rise around the world. It seems anti-Christian forces are becoming stronger each day. In these troubled times, the need for Christians to unite in brotherly love, mutual understanding, and support has never been greater. I received this from a friend. Perhaps there's something in it that will encourage you.

Why Go To Church? A Church attender wrote a letter to the editor of a newspaper and complained that it made no sense to go to church every Sunday. "I've gone for 30 years now," he wrote, "and in that time I have heard something like 3,000 sermons. But for the life of me, I can't remember a single one of them. So, I think I'm wasting my time and the pastors are wasting theirs by giving us sermons at all." This started a real controversy in the "Letters to the Editor" column, much to the delight of the editor. It went on for weeks until someone wrote this clincher: "I've been married for 30 years now. In that time my wife has cooked some 32,000 meals. But, for the life of me, I cannot recall the entire menu for a single one of those meals. But I do know this. They all nourished me and gave me the strength I needed to do my work. If my wife had not given me these meals, I would be physically dead today. Likewise, if I had not gone to church for nourishment, I would be spiritually dead today!

There are many blessings and great spiritual nourishment awaiting you in your local church. If you are currently active in your church, you don't need me to remind you of this truth. However, if you are not in the habit of attending Bible study and worship, I encourage you to get involved. God will be pleased and you will definitely be strengthened and encouraged—and God will give you opportunity to encourage others.

Apr 24

Chuckle: *A man went to the bank and asked to see the man who arranges loans.*

"I'm sorry, sir," said the cashier, "the loan arranger is out to lunch."

"Then," asked the man, "can I please speak to Tonto?"

Quote: *"It is only the great sinner who can do the two things of hating the sin and loving the sinner, the other sort only hates the sin."* ~ J.B. Yeats

Warts and All

"Therefore he is able to save completely those who come to God through him, because he always lives to intercede for them" (Hebrews 7:25 NIV).

I once read about a British nobleman who sat to have his formal portrait painted. After it was finished, he saw a most remarkable likeness. But instead of complimenting the artist, he said, "you didn't paint the wart!" The artist responded, "But, sir, I think you are more attractive without it. Don't you think so?" The nobleman answered, "Paint me as I am—wart and all!"

Aren't you thankful that you are precious and beautiful in the eyes of God, even with all the imperfections—warts—that sin has imprinted upon your heart and life? As did the nobleman, recognizing and accepting our imperfections gives evidence of a certain level of maturity before God. But God's grace is sufficient to save even the most sinful and unattractive, wart-covered reprobate among us; and it is only after we begin to see ourselves in such a hopeless condition that God is able to work His miracle of grace in our lives. After you have experienced God's grace even with your "warts and all," you are now much more willing to accept, overlook, and forgive imperfections in others.

We all have "warts." We all mess up. We all make mistakes. We all sin (see Romans 3:23). When you acknowledge your faults and transgressions, one response is to harbor a sense of guilt and regret; and refuse to forgive yourself. Sometimes the most difficult person to forgive is yourself, because you may feel unworthy of God's love, grace, and forgiveness—and the forgiveness of others. Or, on the other hand, you can recognize your shortcomings and remember that God loves you—warts and all—and He showed that love in that while you were still a sinner, Christ died for you (see Romans 5:8).

Speaking of God's love, I think it was Max Lucado who said, "If God carried a wallet, your picture would be in it." If you know Christ as Savior, when God looks at your picture, I'm sure He doesn't see the warts/sins because they have all been covered by the blood of Jesus. Our passage tells us that our Advocate, our High Priest, our Mediator, our Lord Jesus Christ, is right now making intercession for you and me and pleading our case before the Father—with not a single wart in sight. Praise!!

Apr 25

Chuckle: *The pastor search committee was interviewing candidates for the church. "What kind of man do you want?" asked one minister.*

The chairman said, "We want a preacher who has never been to the Holy Land, who cannot sing solos, and who has never studied Greek!"

Quote: *"I think, therefore I am."* ~ Descartes; French Philosopher; 1596 – 1650

We Are What We Think

"For the word of God is full of living power. It is sharper than the sharpest knife, cutting deep into our innermost thoughts and desires. It exposes us for what we really are. Nothing in all creation can hide from him" (Hebrews 4:12-13 NLT).

The very thoughts that we entertain are important to God. A biblical concept that was particularly difficult for me grasp is that, in God's sight, sinful thoughts can be just as condemning as sinful actions. You may remember Jesus' words during His Sermon on the Mount concerning adultery. *"But I say, anyone who even looks at a woman with lust in his eye has already committed adultery with her in his heart"* (Matthew 5:28 NLT). *"For out of the overflow of the heart, the mouth speaks"* (Matthew 12:34b NIV). *"For as he thinketh in his heart, so is he"* (Proverbs 23:7 KJV).

As damaging as an impure heart and ungodly thoughts can be to our relationship with God and our ultimate happiness; pure, positive, and holy thoughts provide a basis for godly actions that are pleasing to God. Godly thoughts also provide us a healthy, happy, and beautiful outlook on life. Jesus said,

"Blessed, Happy, are the pure in heart, for they will see God" (Matthew 5:8 NIV).

In our quote of the day, Descartes emphasized the truth that we are what we think. Here are some amazing words from the deaf and blind Helen Keller, *"Mine has been the limited experience of one who lives in a world without color and without sound. But ever since my student days I have had a joyous certainty that my physical handicaps were not an essential part of my being, since they were not in any way a part of my mind. This faith was confirmed when I came to Descartes' maxim. 'I think, therefore I am.'*

Those five emphatic words waked something in me that has never slept. I knew then that my mind could be a positive instrument of happiness, bridging over the dark, silent void with concepts of a vibrant, light-flooded happiness. I learned that it is possible for us to create light and sound and order within us, no matter what calamity may befall us in the outer world."

"As selfishness and complaint pervert and cloud the mind, so love with its joy clears and sharpens the vision." ~ Helen Keller.

The condition of our hearts and our innermost thoughts will determine who we really are before God. *"I think, therefore I am."*

Apr 26

Chuckle: *"Be careful about reading health books. You may die of a misprint."* ~ Mark Twain

Quote: *"Judge each day not by the harvest you reap but by the seeds you plant."* ~ William Ward

Uniquely You

"You knitted me together in my mother's womb. I praise you, for I am fearfully and wonderfully made; your works are wonderful, I know that full well" (Psalm 139:13-14 NIV).

Somewhere I read an estimate that the chances of another person being exactly like you or me are one in trillions. However, if I understand the Scriptures, it is impossible for another person to be exactly like someone else. God created each of us as "one of a kind" and has described our uniqueness. God's hand was on you while you were being formed in your mother's womb and He had a plan for your life. *"With your own eyes you saw my body being formed. Even before I was born, you had written in your book everything I would do"* (Psalm 139:16 CEV).

God saw us and knew us when we were embryos, and He has formed us and planned our days on this earth from the start. I cannot understand how some Christians can be okay with aborting, for the convenience of the mother, a life that God knows from the moment of conception. Each life is special and precious to the Creator who has a purpose and plan for that life.

Your personality traits and abilities that God has given you make you unique among all others. You may think God wasn't very careful when He made you because of your perceived flaws and weaknesses. However, your every characteristic contributes to your uniqueness and the perfection God sees in you. You are as valuable to God as any other human being on earth regardless of your appearance, social status, wealth, or personal skills. The Bible tells us there is no favoritism with God.

God loves your uniqueness in the same way you love each of your children even though each one is totally different and unique in his/her own way. Their uniqueness becomes more precious to you as they grow and develop. Today I hope you will rejoice and celebrate because you have been so wonderfully and uniquely made by God Himself. In your rejoicing pledge to carry out the great plan God has for your life. He will strengthen your every weakness and make you strong in Him.

One of the most amazing aspects of God creating each of us is that He has given us the freedom to choose spiritual life in Christ, or death without Him. Jesus said, *"I am the way and the truth and the life. No one comes to the Father except through me"* (John 14:6 NIV).

Apr 27

Chuckle: *Son to dad watching TV: "Dad, tell me again how when you were a kid you had to walk all the way across the room to change the channel."*

Ponder This: *"Nothing spoils a confession like repentance."* ~ Anatole France

Toes and Woes

"Woe to me!" I cried. "I am ruined! For I am a man of unclean lips, and I live among a people of unclean lips, and my eyes have seen the King, the Lord Almighty" (Isaiah 6:5 NIV).

If you participated in a church worship service last Sunday, what lasting impact did that experience have on the way you live? Did it cause you to change your lifestyle? Did the preaching of God's Word pierce and convict your heart of sin in your life? Did you respond to God's message in a way that has changed your attitudes and your daily activities? Was your life changed by being in God's presence? The answers to these questions are terribly important to the acceptability of our worship in the eyes of God.

Years ago I became aware of something that has caused me to evaluate my own worship and to better understand how people participate in and react to public worship. At the end of worship services, I noticed that some people would routinely tell the pastor how much they had enjoyed the service and say something like this, "Pastor, that was a great message. You really stepped on my <u>toes</u>." Then I noticed that some of those same people walked out of the worship service and seemingly never thought about it again. Being in God's presence did not result in observable changes in their behavior. It's as if having their toes stepped on each week was the extent of their worship.

Now let's look at Isaiah's attitude when he found himself in the presence of Almighty God. When confronted with God's Holiness, he saw himself as an unworthy and sinful person in desperate need of God's mercy and forgiveness. He was so distraught about his condition that he exclaimed, *"Woe to me for I am a man of unclean lips."* When we find ourselves in a worship service and become aware that the God of the universe is present, that His Holy Spirit is working, and that He is speaking His Word to us through the music, the message, and prayers, our first reaction should be like Isaiah's, "Lord I am unworthy to be in your presence. Please forgive me of my sins and cleanse my unclean lips/life, and help me adjust my life to bring honor and glory to your name."

Does your total experience leave you feeling good and happy, or is there also a time of self-examination and repentance that makes you feel anything but happy? You see, it is not enough to go to church each Sunday, enjoy the music, listen to the message, and tell the pastor he stepped on your toes.

Every worship experience—every encounter with God— should change us from the inside out. We should go into every service with open hearts, anticipating what God wants to do in us. We should recognize that being in God's presence and hearing His voice should change our lives forever. If our lives are not changed after being in God's presence, we best find out why. Is it "Toes" or "Woes" when you go to church?

Apr 28

Chuckle: *Sunday School Teacher: "Why did Moses wander in the desert for forty years?"*

Ginny: "Because he was too stubborn to stop and ask for directions."

Quote: *"Today is a most unusual day, because we have never lived it before; we will never live it again; it is the only day we have."* ~ William Arthur Ward

Today's Opportunities

"Be very careful, then, how you live—not as unwise but as wise, making the most of every opportunity" (Ephesians 5:15 NIV).

Today's opportunities are the only ones we have with certainty. Let's review some other verses that bear out this truth: *"This is the day that the Lord has made; let us rejoice and be glad in it"* (Psalm 118:24 NIV). *"Do not worry about tomorrow, for tomorrow will worry about itself"* (Matthew 6:34 NIV). *"Do not boast about tomorrow, for you do not know what a day may bring"* (Proverbs 27:1 NIV). *"Why, you do not even know what will happen tomorrow"* (James 4:14 NIV).

Rather than living in the past or worrying about tomorrow, we should live for the joys of today. You can miss today, but you can't live tomorrow today. James 3 warns us about being overconfident about the future. We should plan for the future, but realize the future is dependent upon God's will. We have no promise of tomorrow—only today.

Moses stood before the Red Sea with the Egyptians at his back. The people asked, "Why didn't we stay in Egypt?" They were living in the past. Moses answered them, *"Do not be*

247

afraid. Stand firm and you will see the deliverance the Lord will bring you today" (Exodus 14:13 NIV).

God only promises today. Jesus taught us to pray, *"Give us this day our daily bread."* Some of us are so concerned about how we will live in the future, we can't enjoy today. This is the day the Lord has made, and He made it for you. The sun came up, you are alive—rejoice and take full advantage of God's gift—today.

At age 66, Harlan Sanders was broke. But being a today person and, using his mother's recipe, he opened a restaurant in Salt Lake City. Today, franchises all over America now sell Kentucky Fried Chicken. We are still licking our fingers. . . . At 66, when most of us are saying, "Oh well, not much of my life is left," Harlan Sanders lived for today. *"Today, if you hear his voice, do not harden your hearts"* (Hebrews 3:7 NIV). Listen each day for God's voice and pray that He will show you how you can bless someone today.

"Now is the time for God's favor, now is the day of salvation" (2 Corinthians 6:2 NIV). Do you ever plan to get right with God? If so, do it today. *"Seek the Lord while He may be found; Call on Him while He is near"* (Isaiah 55:6 NIV). Do you plan to make your marriage better? Start today. Witness to someone today. Restore fractured relationships today. Just say, "I want to be a today person. Jesus always brings us back to today, the only day that matters." Tomorrow will never come.

Apr 29

Chuckle: *"I just got skylights put in my place. The people who live above me are furious."*

Quote: *"All the events in your life are a mirror image of your thoughts."* ~ Unknown Source

Thoughts Are Key

"Finally, brothers, whatever is true, whatever is noble, whatever is right, whatever is pure, whatever is lovely, whatever is admirable—If anything is excellent or praiseworthy—think on such things" (Philippians 4:8-9 NIV).

Some people carry key rings containing many keys. Sometimes they fumble trying to find the right key to open the door leading to where they want to go. We can find ourselves frustrated and anxious in such situations. The right key is the answer. The same is true in our spiritual life. We may search and search to find the key to a closer walk and fellowship with God. The key that Paul shows us will help us get from where we are to where we can realize God's promise of peace and fulfilment.

Paul's key is to "think on such things" as he enumerated in our passage. In other words, he tells us to allow only godly thoughts to fill our minds. These words mean to ponder, dwell, and concentrate on such praiseworthy things. If we want to draw nearer to God, the thoughts we entertain will make the difference. This is because our actions will reflect the thoughts of our hearts. Holy thoughts will result in holy words and actions. Jesus said, *"For out of the overflow of the heart the mouth speaks"* (Matthew 12:34b NIV).

This theme is emphasized in Romans 12:2b NLT, *"but let*

God transform you into a new person by changing the way you think." When we think on true, noble, right, pure, lovely, and admirable things, our lives will reflect such thoughts and we will draw closer to God.

As Christians, we know it is the Holy Spirit who guides us to entertain godly thoughts. It's only when the Holy Spirit renews, re-educates, and redirects our thoughts that we become truly transformed. As we are controlled by the Holy Spirit, we will be on the offensive to fill our minds with wholesome thoughts and values totally different from those of the world.

Do you have problems with impure thoughts and daydreams? If so, you might consider what you are putting into your mind from TV, books, conversations, movies, and magazines; and replace the polluted input with wholesome material. Above all, study God's Word and pray—asking God to help you focus your mind on what is good and pure. Then you will be motivated to put your wholesome thoughts into godly words and actions. In the process, you will grow spiritually and draw closer to your Lord.

Apr 30

Chuckle: *"When you are dissatisfied and would like to go back to youth, think of Algebra."* ~ Will Rogers"

Jesus said, *"Blessed are those who hunger and thirst after righteousness, for they will be filled"* (Matthew 5:6 NIV).

Thirsting for God

"As the deer pants for streams of water, so my soul pants for you, O God. My soul thirsts for God, for the living God. When can I go and meet with God?" (Psalm 42:1-2 NIV).

Dotse and I enjoy sitting on our back porch and watching deer that graze and bed down on our lawn. They are fun to watch but they certainly are destructive to plants and shrubs. Here in Central Texas, we normally have several months of hot dry weather each summer. The deer sometimes become desperate for water and we see them drinking from fish ponds, bird baths, etc. You can actually see them panting from the heat and the need for water. Their severe need causes them to take extreme measures to quench their thirsts.

In our passage, the psalmist so yearned for God's intimate presence in his life that he compared his longing for God to that of a panting deer's thirst for water. What an amazing testimony by the writer of this Psalm who was likely in exile somewhere to the north of Mount Hermon. He was longing to be on the mountain with God Himself. Evidently, he felt that God was far away, and not available to him. He was in a desert with no way to quench his thirst.

Have there been times when you have felt that God was far away? I think every Christian has, or will, have such an experience. When we feel this way, we need to remember that

God does not move away from us—we move away from Him. It may be that some sin has gained a foothold in your live which creates a breach in fellowship between you and God. You may have allowed something to become a higher priority than your relationship with the living Lord. A warning signal is the absence of a thirst and yearning for God. But the important thing is to recognize your condition and draw near to God out of a deep personal need for His forgiving, healing, and comforting presence in your life. As you draw near to God, He will draw near to you.

Jesus said to the Samaritan woman at the well, *"If you knew the gift of God and who it is that asks you for a drink, you would have asked him and he would have given you living water"* (John 4:10 NIV). Jesus continued, *"but whoever drinks the water I give him will never thirst. Indeed, the water I give him will become in him a spring of water welling up to eternal life"* (John 4:14 NIV). Can you say with the psalmist, *"My soul thirsts for God, for the living God"*?

About the Author:

Jerry Stratton grew up as the son of a Baptist minister in the beautiful mountains of Northwest Arkansas. He is a graduate of Ouachita Baptist University, Arkadelphia, Arkansas; and Baylor University, Waco, Texas. He served in the U.S. Army for a total of 30 years and retired in December, 1984.

Upon retirement from the army, Jerry sensed God's call to vocational ministry. In his 28 years of ministry, he has served as minister of education and administration, director of missions, pastor, and interim pastor. For the past eight years, he has published a daily devotional via e-mail and his personal blog. In addition to his internet devotional ministry, Jerry continues to minister through his local church and substitute preaching.

Jerry and his wife, Dotse, met at Ouachita Baptist University. The celebrated 61 years of marriage in August, 2015 and make their home in Copperas Cove, Texas. Their two wonderful children have blessed them with six fantastic grandchildren.